1968

s book may be kept

WATERMARKS IN PAPER

IN HOLLAND
ENGLAND
FRANCE
ETC.

IN THE XVII AND XVIII CENTURIES
AND THEIR INTERCONNECTION

Rags make paper

PAPER MAKES MONEY

MONEY MAKES BANKS

Banks make Loans

Loans make beggars

Beggers make rags

WATERMARKS IN PAPER

IN HOLLAND, ENGLAND,
FRANCE, ETC., IN THE XVII
AND XVIII CENTURIES AND
THEIR INTERCONNECTION

BY

W. A. CHURCHILL

MENNO HERTZBERGER & Co. — AMSTERDAM

© 1935. Menno Hertzberger & Co, Amsterdam

This book or parts thereof should not be reproduced
in any form by print, photoprint, microfilm, or any
other means without written permission from the publishers.

First published	1935
Reprinted photo-mechanically	1965
Third impression	1967

PRINTED IN THE NETHERLANDS
Krips Reprint Company, Meppel

HOLLAND

(1) The paper industry in Europe and in Holland is one of the results of wars. The Arabs who defeated a Chinese army near Samarkand in the middle of the 8th century, learnt the art of paper-making from their Chinese prisoners and gradually introduced it throughout their empire, until finally it reached Spain in the middle of the 12th century. The capture of Antwerp (which was a great paper centre in the 16th century) by the forces of Austria, drove its paper merchants north to Holland. The earliest mention of national paper-making in Holland was contained in a decree (2) signed by the Earl of Leicester in 1586 authorizing Hans van Aelst and Jan Luipart to manufacture paper near Dordrecht. At this time Holland (3) was invaded by Spain and Austria, and being unable to resist alone offered the sovereignty of the Netherlands to Queen Elizabeth, who did not accept, but sent a military force under the Earl of Leicester. He was appointed head of the state, and as such he signed state papers. When the armies of Louis XIV invaded Guelderland (1671) the paper mills of that province were transferred for greater safety to the Zaan district near Amsterdam. It was from here that a great paper industry came into being and became world famous. It will be seen therefore that wars — "the malady of princes" — have brought in their train blessings without which the printed word could not have reached the millions as it does to-day.

The trade secret was so well kept by the Chinese, that the invention of paper making in Europe might have been delayed until the 18th century, (4) when two or three observers noticed that a paper-like substance was (5) formed by the action of wasps when making their nests, and that a paper-like film rises to the surface of stagnant waters.

[5]

According to Stoppelaar, the oldest paper found in the archives of
Holland is dated 1346, and is preserved at The Hague. In his monograph
(6)   on old paper in Holland, he gives 271 reproductions of watermarks, nearly
(7)   all of which figure in Briquet's Dictionary of Watermarks. The watermarks show that the earliest paper came from Italy, France, Switzerland
and Germany. The watermark of a windmill that appears on the cover
of the monograph is of French origin.

At the beginning of the 17th century, Holland imported printing and
writing paper from Germany, France, Switzerland and Genoa, because
at that time no fine white paper was manufactured in the country. The
chief distributing centres were Antwerp and Cologne, but as prices became
too high, Dutch middlemen or factors went to France in the Angoumois
district early in the 17th century and had paper made for the Dutch
market. At first the paper bore well-known French or foreign marks,
mostly described by Briquet, but later they bore Dutch marks with
French countermarks. From this time on Amsterdam developed a world
market for the distribution of paper. In 1635 the coat-of-arms of Amsterdam begins to appear as a watermark on paper. This seems to be the
first Dutch watermark, but it was made in France alone, and we only
know that the first maker's initials were "I. M." From this time onwards
(8)   paper with variations of the watermark of Amsterdam was made at first
in numerous French mills and later in Dutch mills. A specimen has even
been discovered that was made in Genoa.

Amsterdam began to export paper to England and elsewhere in the
beginning of the 17th century. There were factors or buying agents for the
(3)   home product, and for the produce of Germany and France. In the early
part of the 17th century German paper was imported through a "Company"
called Lodewyk Coningh, Albert Jaso & Co. This Company supplied
much paper with the following watermark:

The letters are the initials of Cornelis and Anna van Lockhorst,
members of the Company. In 1634 the Company got into difficulties,

and from that date the import of German paper gradually ceased. French paper replaced it, especially for printing. Home and foreign paper was handled by factors established at Amsterdam, but French paper was handled by factors established in France, mainly in the province of Angoumois.

The success of Amsterdam as a world distributor of paper, including the produce of France, aroused French opposition. The French Government did its utmost to protect national industry and to place obstacles in the way of Dutch competition.

The Angoumois district, which was one of the most important producers of paper in France, came under the control of foreign capital, (6) mainly Dutch. Many of the master paper-makers and their workmen (9) were Protestants or Huguenots, and on the revocation of the Edict of Nantes (1685) when non-Catholics were persecuted and expelled from France, many of them emigrated to England and Holland. The Dutch factors who had been established in France for upwards of half a century were obliged to withdraw, as they were not Catholics. The blow intended for the Dutch recoiled on the French industry and benefited that of Holland, where the industry became concentrated from this time on, and moreover was reinforced by the addition of skilled immigrants from France. Until 1685 the Dutch were mainly paper merchants, but henceforward they became manufacturers as well, and even supplied France and Italy — their former sources — with the finest paper obtainable.

Although the highest standard of quality was reached in Holland during the 18th century and an increasing demand for Dutch paper arose in various countries of Europe and the Levant, the majority of books published in Holland during this period were printed on French paper. At this (10) time Amsterdam was one of the principal printing centres of the world. In a collection of 1000 printed placards or official notices, measuring about 20″ × 17″, for the period from 1618 to 1797, the foreign and Dutch sheets amount to only 36, all the rest being French, which shows a marked preference for French printing paper.

(11) A curious illustration of this preference may be noticed in a work published by Messrs A. Blussé & Zoon of Dordrecht, when they wished to include in their series of technological text books, a work describing the manufacture of paper. The writer, named Kasteleyn of Amsterdam,

[7]

instead of producing an original Dutch work, which he might have done, gave a translation of the French manual by De Lalande. It was printed on French paper and published by Messrs. Blussé in 1792 and dedicated by them to Messrs. Blauw & Briel, renowned paper-makers of Wormerveer with whom they had enjoyed friendly and commercial relations for many years.

This preference for French paper confirms the opinion of the late Mr. J. W. Enschedé, an authority on paper and printing, who asserted that Holland never excelled in the manufacture of printing paper, and that the best product was used for writing. On the other hand it must be admitted that Dutch paper has been successfully used in various countries for printed works, and excellent maps and atlases have been engraved on (12) Dutch paper. One must turn to France for evidence of Dutch superiority. Towards the middle of the 18th century, the Inspector of Manufactures in France recommanded Vimal of Auvergne (his watermark was a pig, being an (13) allusion to his name) as one of those best qualified to maintain the superiority of his produce, if he would only transform his plant in accordance with the Dutch process. Merchants had such a high opinion of him that they begged him to imitate Dutch paper, with the same laid lines and watermarks as made in Holland, so that the public who were prejudiced against the native article should no longer refuse it. In describing the Dutch industry in 1762 De Lalande said that "although Dutch paper is finer than French, it lacks the finish of the latter. Dutch paper has a finer, smoother and more transparent appearance than ours. This is due to the uniform fineness of their linen rags, which are carefully selected and not mixed. Dutch paper is thicker and better prepared than ours, because their moulds are deeper, and because pulping by Dutch cylinders is superior to that by stampers. Moreover, Dutch workmen work with more care and deliberation than our workmen are accustomed to. The wealth of their paper-makers, the thrift of their inhabitants and the power of their finances combine to make their mills more efficient than ours. What has been said, however, concerning the properties of Dutch paper applies only to the superfine qualities, such as: large horn, Pro Patria and the arms of England and Venice. There are many sorts that are inferior to our paper of Auvergne, such as: the double fine crown and double (14) fine "écu" (arms of France) made at Thiers, Ambert and Annonay".

[8]

The Almanac of Troyes for the year 1776 publishes the following advertisement: "Sieur Bouvet established a very fine paper factory a few years ago at Estissac, a village situated four leagues from Troyes, where he (15) manufactures superfine white and blue papers in the Dutch style." La Rochefoucauld's crest became Bouvet's watermark.

Mr. J. G. Honig of Koog aan de Zaan has a collection of old paper wrappers, one of which bears the following wording: "Papier fin fait par Jacques Corneille Miel au Moulin de la Ruche à Miel." J. C. Miel is no other than Jacob Cornelisz Honig, and the "moulin" was the celebrated Golden Beehive at Zaandyk. The French wording was probably intended for paper exported to France.

For a long time fine printing in France was made on "papier de Hollande", but it is known that much of this product was made in France to satisfy the prejudice of persons who admire anything that is foreign. It is possible that the designation "papier de Hollande" originated from the fact that superfine paper was manufactured long ago in Angoumois with Dutch watermarks for the Dutch market.

The first important mill in Holland was erected in 1665 by Pieter van der Ley at Zaandyk, and his watermarks are to be seen frequently in prints and MS. in Holland and England. The firm, which lasted over one hundred years, was followed by a number of other celebrated mills such as those of the Honighs, van Gerrevinks, Villedary, Blauw & Briel, Kool, Rogge, Pannekoek, and Cramer & Co. In the watermarks in paper made by these firms one has clear evidence that much of their produce was made expressly for the British market. These watermarks include Dutch marks in conjunction with the royal monograms of William III, Anne, and the Georges; they include also the Britannia mark, and the coat-of-arms of England and London together with the names of Dutch mills, in addition to those of English merchants and even paper-makers, such as Whatman and Portal.

(6) Until 1670 Dutch paper had not the strength of French paper. The first to equal French paper was made by Pieter van der Ley about 1675. At the end of the 17th century there were sixty mills in the Zaan district and 115 in the Veluwe. Peter the Great visited two paper mills on the Zaan named "De Kok" and "De Walvisch", and had a mill constructed in Russia on the Dutch model. In the 18th century Holland imported French

[9]

(6) printing paper from Bordeaux, La Rochelle, St. Malo and Morlaix.
The accompanying illustration depicts the stone carving representing the interior of a paper mill, that was fixed to the house built in 1649 for Pieter de Haak, paper merchant of Amsterdam. The house was pulled down in 1908, and the carving is now in the Academy of Fine Arts in Amsterdam. This is the oldest representation of a Dutch paper mill. The wheel in this carving is a water wheel, and therefore represents a Veluwe mill, because in this district mills were driven by water power,
(16) whereas in the Zaan district they were driven by wind.

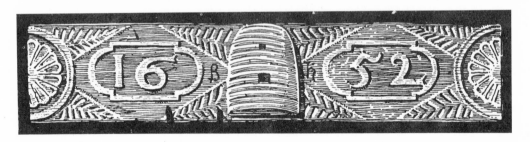

The lower picture represents a wood carving over the door of the house of the former owners of the Golden Beehive mill, one of whose
(17) watermarks was a beehive. This mark has been imitated very much in
(18) other countries, particularly in Germany. The picture was taken from a work by Mr. Gerrit Jan Honig, a descendant of the famous paper-makers of that name.

[10]

A Dutch Ordinance of 1636 mentions the following sorts of paper:

		Duty per ream
Lombardy vellum		Gulden 30
Royal and Elephant	(German)	15
Post	,,	10
FFF	,,	
Strasburg Lily WR	,,	
Cardinal		
Flower		7
Toren-yser (Thurneysen)	Swiss	
Two Bears	,,	
I. D.		
Middelhuys (Heusler)	,,	
(16) Small Lily		5
Crozier of Basel		
C/O/A of Saxony		
Dolphin		4
Eagle		
Cardoes (Cartridge)	French	10
Pot	,,	3

Chronological list of watermarks:

1629	P. Düring
,,	Lion and man
,,	Toradel (Tower on breast of eagle)
1633	Flower (German)
1636	Strasburg Lily
,,	FFF
,,	Arms of Cardinal
,,	't Huys H. Crans (Heusler)
,,	Toren-yser (Thurneysen)
,,	P. P.
,,	Two Bears

(16) 1636 Bartels flower
　　 ,,　　 I. D.
　　 ,,　　 W. R. (Wendelin Riehel)
　　 ,,　　 Crozier of Basel
　　 ,,　　 Saxon shield
　　 ,,　　 Dolphin
　　 ,,　　 Elephant
　　 ,,　　 Pot
　 1643　 Horn
　　 ,,　　 Snake
　　 ,,　　 Foolscap
　　 ,,　　 Gros bon Cardinal
　 1648　 "à la serviette"
　 1666　 Post paper (Italian)
　 1670　 Amsterdam C/o/a V. G. (Van Gangelt)
　　 ,,　　 Foolscap G. B.
　 1664　 Post rider or Postilion

DUTCH PAPER-MAKERS

Date of MSS., Prints or Decrees.		Locality of mills
1740	Aalders, Jacobus	Groningen
1628/32	Aelst, Andries van	near Arnhem
1592	Aelst, Frans van	near Arnhem
1628/32	Aelst, Frans van	
1618	Aelst, Gerrit van	Eerbeek mill
1586	Aelst, Hans van	near Dordrecht, first mill in Holland
1592	Aelst, Jan van	Veluwe
1628	Aelst, Liefke van	Veluwe
1628	Aelst, Lyntje van	Veluwe
1623	Aelst, Lodewyk van	Apeldoorn
1654	Aelst, Lodewyk van	Beekbergen
1602	Alleman, Hans	Overveen
1827	Ameshoff, J. H.	
1632	Arendz, Hendrik	Zaandam
1734—1800	Backer, Pieter Roelofz.	Zaandyk, Zemelzak mill
1835	Benthem, S. van	
1777—82	Berends, J.	
1724—1825	Blauw & Briel	Wormerveer & Zaandyk
1733—1827	Blauw, Dirk — & Co.	Oude Blauw mill
1822	Blauw, De Erven D.	
1586	Bois, Jan Jacobz. du	Alkmaar
to 1841	Breet, Jacob & Klaas	Zaandyk
1813	Brouwer, G. & I. — & Co.	
1740	Brouwer, Gerrit	Veluwe
1810	Brouwer, H. — & Co.	
1808—40	Brouwer, P.	
1839	Charro, H. F. de — & Zn.	The Hague
1616	Cornelisz, Jacob	Zaandyk, De Kauwer mill
1711	Cramer, Bernardus	Ootmarsum, now Berghuizer Papierfabriek at Hattem

1734—1796	Cramer, Symon	Zaandyk, De Visser mill
	Delden, D. van	Rosendaal
1839	Delden, D. van	Loenen
1669	Dell, Nicolaes	Amsterdam
1721	Dercks, J.	
	Desjardyn	
1604	Deyman, Ysbrandt	Amsterdam
	Durandaus, J.	
1740	Engelse, Michiel	Zaandyk, De Hoop mill
1734	Engelse, Gerrit	Zaandyk, De Gans mill
	Feuilletau de Bruyn & Co.	
1790	Forsten & Co.	
1607	Fredericksz	Amsterdam
1803	Gelder, van — Schouten & Co.	Wormer
1855	Gelder, van — Zonen	Wormer
1601	Gent, Adriaen Lievensz van	
1690—1819	Gerrevink, Lubertus van	Egmond a/d Hoef, Phoenix mill
1730	Gerrevink, Lucas van	Alkmaar, Phoenix mill
1733	Gerrevink, Abram & Isaac	Egmond a/d Hoef
1596	Gillis, Gregorie	Middelburg
	Goey or Goei, H. D.	
1775—94	Goey or Goei, M. de	
1609	Hackforth, Gerard	Barneveld
1794	Hendricks & Zoon	
1653	Hendricksen, Cornelis	Loenen
1621	Hendriksz, Hendrik	Amsterdam
1603	Hendriksz, Jan	Amsterdam
1787	Hessels, J.	
1845	Hesselink, A. & I.	
1810	Hesselink, Gerrit	
1685	Heses, Sons of J. T.	Schoorl
1823	Heyden, van — & Co.	
1758?	Hissink, W.	

1609	Hoeve, Pieter v/d	Alkmaar
1683—1856	Honig, Cornelis & Jacob	Zaandyk, Herderskind mill
1734	Honig, Cornelis Adriaan	Zaandyk
1675—1902	Honig, Cornelis A. & Jan	Zaandyk, De Vergoldene Bykorf mill
1680	Honig, Jan Adriaan & Cornelis	
	Honig & Co.	
to 1894	Honig, Jan — & Co.	Last owners of J. v/d Ley's mill Fortuyn at Zaandyk
1702	Honig, G. — & Zoon	Zaandyk
1737—87	Honig, Jan — & Zoon	Zaandyk
	Houtum, Joh. van	Arnhem & Apeldoorn
1770	Hoysing, H. C.	
1774	Hummen, I.	Veluwe
XVII C	Jacobsz, Jan	Alkmaar
1601	Jacobsz, Willem	Alkmaar, De Dikke Guurt mill
1603	Jansz, Hendrik	Amsterdam
1617	Jansz, Jacob	
1605	Jansz, Jan	Amsterdam
1613	Jansz, Jan	Ugchelen, near Apeldoorn
1740	Jong, Jan de	Zaanland
1792	Jonker, W. A.	
1796	Kamphuysen, H.	Molecaten
1605	Keyns, Rens Dirksz. v/d	Schagen
1740	Kelder, Cornelis Jansz	Zaanland
1813	Kempen, v. — & Co.	
1791—1813	Kloppenburg	
1791—1810	Kloppenburg, J.	
1808	Koldewyn, H.	
	Koning & Desjardyn	
1728—1800	Kool, Jan	

1821	Kool, I. — & Co.	
1788	Korff & De Vries	
1771	Kouwenhoven	
to 1796	Kouwenhoven, Adriaan & Jan	Zaandyk
1711	Kremer, see Cramer	
	Krantz de Charro & Co.	
to 1788	Lakeman, Jan	Zaandyk
	Ledeboer, I. H.	Velp
1601	Lenaerts, Adriaan	Amsterdam
1703—1894	Ley, Jan v/d	Zaandyk, Fortuyn mill
1740	Ley, Jan, Claes & Aris v/d	Zaandyk, Fortuyn mill
1665—1765	Ley, Pieter v/d	Wormerveer, Wever mill
1698—1815	Ley, van der	
1832	Lier, M. v. — & Zoon	The Hague
1586	Luipaert, Jan	
1799	Meyrink, C. I.	
1807	Middelink, I. T.	
XVIII C	Mos, Jan	
XVII C	Nanning, Albrecht	Dordrecht
1795	Neerdorp	
XVIII C	Niello	
1808	Niello, De Weduwe F. A. — & Co.	Amsterdam
	Nieuwland & Kloppenburg	
1734—1788	Note, Klaas Jansz.	Zaandyk
1795	Oorspronk, F. V.	
1613—26	Orges or Orgel, Martin	Ugchelen
1625	Orges or Orgel, Paul Martens	
XVIII C	Otterloo, W.	
	Palm & Zoon	Veluwe
1740	Pannekoek, Abram	
1777	Pannekoek, G.	
1848	Pannekoek, G. J. W.	

1717	Pannekoek, Klaas, or Nico-laas	Heelsum
1772	Pannekoek, W. & C.	
1808	Pannekoek, W. W. & H.	
	Pasman, B. H.	
1610/25	Pieterz, Gerrit	P. v/d Ley made paper with letters "G. P." in 1673
1628	Poel, Pieter & Abr. v/d	
1808	Printz, Joh.	
1841	Proost, I.	
1751	Raket, Hendrik	Zaandyk
1796	Reyers, Z.	
1605	Rinnegum, Jan Jansz	Alkmaar
	Roelofs, G.	
1704—1803	Rogge, Adriaan	Zaandam
1808	Sande, W. G. v/d	
	Sanders, T. — & Zoon	Apeldoorn
1739—1830	Schoen, Hendrik	Zaandyk, De Herderin mill
1707—43	Schoen, W. H.	
1783—1803	Schouten, Marten van — & Co.	Wormer
1598	Schuren, Jan van	Hattem
1740	Schut, D. I.	Veluwe
1863	Schut, I. K.	
1745	Sebelle, D. — & Wend	
1745	Sebelle, Ketel & Wassenbergh	
1740	Verburg, A.	Groningen
1758	Villedary, Jean	Hattem
1721—47	Vierrevant, Jeers	
1720	Vorsten, N.	Loenen, Veluwe
1790	Vorster, H.	
1796	Vos, A.	
	Vos & Knoops	

1799	Vries, Pieter de — & Comp.	
1779	Wassenbergh	
1840	Wassenbergh & Co.	
	Wend, H. C.	
1790	Wend, H. C. — & Zonen	
1790	Wend & Zonen	
1734—1841	Wessanen, Cornelis Adriaan	Zaandyk
1621	Willemsz, Hendrik	
1739	Wolbrink, Egbert	Schoorl, Roode Hert mill
	Wysmuller, Erve	Amsterdam, still exists

In addition to these names a list compiled in 1740 of about 150 paper-makers of Zaandyk, Egmond, Groningen and the province of Guelderland was published by Mr. G. J. Honig of Koog a/d Zaan in the Nederlandsche Familieblad in 1888, p. 247 et seq.

FRENCH PAPER-MAKERS WHO WORKED FOR THE DUTCH MARKET

Date of MSS., Prints or Not. Acts		Locality
1754—69	Ballande, P.	Agenois
1769	Ballande Cadet	
1744	Barre, Jean	Périgord
1651—62	Bernard, Pierre	Beauvais, Angoumois
1736	Bruin, B.	Angoumois
1749	Brun, Bernard	Angoumois
1661	Chatonet, François	Charente, Rieff mill
1788	Dablan, V.	Angoumois, La Couronne mill
1653	Dalidet, Giles	
1679—1700	Declide, F.	Angoumois, La Courrade mill
1778	Degau, A.	
1603	Demarcillac, F.	Angoumois, Pont des Tables mill
1654—79	Dexmier, P.	Angoumois, La Pallurie mill
XVIII C	Dexmier, Veuve — & F. Declide	Angoumois, La Courrade mill
1747	Dort, J.	
1781	Dumas, A.	
1739—89	Dumas, François	Périgord
1789	Dumas, I. Aîné	
1777	Fouant, M.	Limousin
1766	Frivard	Limousin
1648	Galtier, Pierre	Angoumois, Beauvais mill
1690—1704	Gallet, Georges	
1785	Geofre, I.	
1643—83	George, Claude de	Angoumois, Nersac mill

1758	Gerlou, I.	
1752	Graterole, P.	Limousin
1656—1793	Jardel, Daniel	Périgord, Couze mill
1701—39	Jardel, Francois	Périgord, Couze mill
1687—1772	Jardel, Jean	Dordogne, Creyse mill
1701—42	Jardel Jr., Jean	Périgord, Couze mill
1706—84	Jardel, Raimond	Périgord, De la Poque mill
1669—99	Joly, Antoine	Angoumois, Nersac mill
1699—1715	Joly, Pierre	
	Juilhard, Daniel	Périgord, Fougère mill
	Latache	see André de la Tache
1736	Marchaix	
1739	Marot, F.	Périgord, Couze mill
1759	Marot, P.	
1782	Marot, R.	
1730	Martin	
1748	Nadel, D.	Périgord
1747	Nadal, G.	
1720—83	Perie, D.	Périgord
	Planteau, Estienne	Périgord, Casteljaloux mill
1753	Potuis	Agenois
1778	Prat, P.	
1690	Riflaud, Pierre	Angoumois, La Couronne mill
1788	Riviére, P.	
1684	Rondel	
1638—61	Roulet, Jean	Angoumois, Le Got & L'Abbaye mills
1632	Rousselot, Jean	Angoumois, Pont de Ruelle mill
1650	Sailhan, J.	Périgord, Clausureau mill
1723—50	Tache, Claude André de la	Angoumois, Ruelle mill

1710	Tarnaud, P.	Angoumois, L'Abbaye mill
1765	Tobias, P.	Angoumois
1773	Tomas, P.	Angoumois
1665	Touzeau, Estienne	Angoumois, St. Michel mill
1706—57	Valet, P.	Périgord
1668—1758	Villedary, Jean	Angoumois, Vraichamp, Beauvais and La Couronne mills
1758—1812	Villedary, Jean	Guelderland, Hattem,
1669	Vincent, Isbram	Angoumois, Chantoiseau mill
1781	Vine, D.	

In addition to the above names, about 150 other French paper-makers made paper for the Dutch market, mainly during the 17th century, using various Dutch watermarks and the makers' initials as a countermark.

The name of D. Jardel appears on paper during a period of 137 years, there having been several generations of the same name.

From the records of a law suit between two factors named Abram Janssen and Jacques Salmon, who had both employed Claude de George to make paper for them, it became known that the latter died in 1683, and that paper with his initials, C. D. G., was made after his death. The explanation was that paper with these initials had a great reputation for excellence, and that the widow of C. de George continued to work his mill and to produce equally good paper with the same watermark. Paper with these initials may be found dated as late as 1706.

The name or initials of Jean Villedary as watermarks cover a period of 150 years. The first French paper-maker of this name made paper for four Dutch factors, viz. Abram Janssen, François van Tongeren, Pierre van Tongeren and Gilis van Hoven. The initials I V, of Jean Villedary, appear on a great deal of paper for books and MSS. in the public archives and libraries of England and Holland. They appear also in conjunction with the names and watermarks of Lubertus van Gerrevink, C. & I. Honig, Adriaan Rogge and Van der Ley. The initials I V and L. V. G. together have been found on paper dated from 1736 to 1812. It is not known whether Villedary worked in conjunction with the other Dutch paper-makers, or whether they made use of his initials, which had become a hall-mark of excellence.

FLEMISH AND DUTCH FACTORS OR AGENTS IN FRANCE.

According to notarial acts at Angoulême one can trace, in 1628, the presence there of Girard Verduyn, a Flemish merchant of the city of Amsterdam. He came to buy paper on his own account and for that of Jean Petittau, his partner in Amsterdam. One finds also Laurent van Ravestein of Leyden, and the following established in the faubourg l'Homeau: Abraham Vannezel, Van der Plasten (1650), Van Gangel, Dericq, Jacob and Abraham Janssen. Most of them were domiciled at Angoulême, and became owners of mills. Van Tongeren acquired the Cothier mill in 1721. This is probably Pierre van Tongeren who in 1739 (19) was described as a banker and owner of paper mills at Cothier.

In a paper mill there were three or four categories of people: (a) the owner of the mill, (b) the master paper-maker, (c) the workmen, who number from 30 to 40 persons in a mill with two vats, (d) the middleman or factor, who came between the owner and the paper maker. This individual furnished the funds.

The factor was usually one of those wealthy Flemish and Dutch merchants mentioned above. Although owners of mills they were not manufacturers, but employed master paper-makers to work for them. The function of the factor was to advance the necessary working capital required by the paper-makers; this amounted on an average to 1000 crowns per (19) vat, and was called the "cabal".

LIST OF DUTCH FACTORS OR AGENTS IN FRANCE AND HOLLAND.

1635	Anthony, Nicolaas	} (Amsterdam agents for the home
1635—53	Bartels, Albert	} (production

1661	Beeck, Pieter Joosten	Bought 20,600 reams of paper from Pierre Galtier of Beauvais, Angoumois, between 1661 and 1663
1635	Beyerland, Willem van	Amsterdam agent for home produce
1635	Blauw, Dr. Johan	Amsterdam agent for home produce, also publisher in Amsterdam
1635	Cabillau, Jonas	Rotterdam
1635	Colom, Jacob Aertsz	Amsterdam agent for home produce
1685	Domma, Pieter	Amsterdam, advertised the sale of Italian paper
1644	Gangel, Christophe van	Supplied paper to P. de Haak from La Couronne mill
1639	Haak, Pieter de	In 1666 the Exchange Bank of Amsterdam had an item for his account for fl. 600,000
1640	Haes, Cornelis & Antonie	Father and son, merchants of Amsterdam. In 1643 they imported from Bordeaux: foolscap, post-horn, cardinal & serpent marked paper
1634	Hoven, Gillis van	In partnership with P. de Haak. Factor in France, several mills worked for him in Angoumois.
1635	Holyen, Rombert van	Amsterdam agent for home produce
1593	Jacobsz, Laurens	Amsterdam agent for Lombardy paper
1635—1710	Janssen, Abraham	Factor at Angoulême, Puymoyen mill
1638—73	Janssen, Dirk	Brother of A. Janssen. Owner of

		St. Michel mill 1656, Tudeboeuf mill 1668, l'Abbaye mill 1673
1669	Janssen, Isaac	Factor in France. Hired a mill at La Rochandry near Angoulême
1651	Janssen, Jacob	Factor in France. Hired mills at Maine-Gaignaud and Ruelle, Angoumois
1712	Janssen, Theodore	Factor in France. Hired a mill at l'Abbaye, Angoumois, brother of A. & D. Janssen
1600—34	Jaso, Lodewyk Coningh, Albert — & Co.	Factors in Amsterdam of German paper
1657	Keulen, Gerrit van	Amsterdam agent for home produce
to 1634	Lockhorst, Cornelis & Anna,	of Utrecht, members of firm of L. C. A. Jaso & Co. Importers also of paper from Basle
c 1646	Loten, Dirk	Factor in France. St. Martin mill near Rouen
1653	Mefferd, Pieter	Amsterdam agent for home produce
1628	Petittau, Jean	Amsterdam importer of French paper. Partner of G. Verduyn
1650	Plasten, van der	Factor in France. Mill at l'Homeau, Angoumois
1635	Preys, Boudewyn de	Amsterdam agent for home produce
c 1625	Raephorst, Dr. Matthys Willemsz.	Amsterdam importer of French paper supplied by D. Janssen & G. v. Hoven
1629	Ravenstein, Laurens v.,	of Leyden. Factor in France, at Faubourg l'Homeau. Bought paper from Jean Gros of Angoulême

[24]

1674	Ridder, Laurens de	of Delft
1648—1720	Salmon, Jacques	Factor in France. Mill at Nersac, Angoumois
1700	Sebelle, Paulus	Paper merchant of Amsterdam. A paper wrapper represents his watermarks as a horn in a shield and a postilion blowing a horn; with the following wording: — "Post papier te koop tot Amsterdam". This is in Bagford's Collection at the British Museum.
1700	Til, Jan van	Factor in France
1666—1710	Tongeren, Frans van	Factor in France. Owned mill at Beauvais worked by Jean Villedary; banker as well as mill owner
1750	Tongeren, Jan van	Factor at Angoulême
1721	Tongeren, Pierre van	Factor in France. Owner of Cothier and St. Martin mills, Angoumois, worked by Jean Villedary, banker at Angoulême in 1739, and "Trésorier de France au bureau des Finances de la Généralité de Limoges"
1631	Vannezel, Abraham	Factor in France. Faubourg l'Homeau, Angoumois
1628	Verduyn, Girard,	of Amsterdam, factor at Angoulême
1635	Visscher, Nicolaas	Amsterdam agent for home produce
1633	Walschaert, H.	Amsterdam importer of German paper
1648	Wit, Frederick	Amsterdam paper dealer and engraver. Engraved the ornaments of the Town Hall at Amsterdam in 1665

[25]

NOTES ON SOME OF THE LEADING DUTCH
FACTORS IN FRANCE

In 1635 a number of Dutch factors established themselves at Angoulême, and among them was Abraham Janssen. He owned mills at Puy-moyen and at Nersac, and employed the following paper-makers: Jean Villedary, Claude de George, Jean and François Jardel, P. Salée, Etienne Touzeau and others. Being a man of substance he soon acquired considerable influence, and was appointed "Intendant des Finances de la Généralité de Limoges". In those days people in trade were not allowed to use crests, but gradually a few exceptions were made for eminently successful manufacturers, and Janssen obtained permission to add a crown to his foolscap watermark.

Dirk Janssen, a brother of Abraham Janssen, is described in local notarial acts as a factor at Angoulême and the owner of various mills between 1638 and 1673. There were probably two men of the same name, because in a church at Egmond a/d Hoef there is a tombstone with the inscription: — "Here lies the paper-maker Dirk Janssen who was laid to (20) rest Nov. 25, 1667". (In Dutch).

Jacques Salmon described as "Escuyer, Seigneur des Moulins, Conseiller du Roy, Lieutenant de la Maréchaussée d'Angulesme", owned a mill at Nersac and employed Claude de George, paper-maker, until his death in 1683. In 1686 Salmon endeavoured by recourse to law to restrain Abraham Janssen from imitating his watermark which partly consisted of the letters C D G the initials of the famous Claude de George. Evidence was furnished showing that Abraham Janssen had injured the plaintiff in the manner complained of, but the lawsuit does not seem to have been concluded. Salmon did not obtain any redress and Janssen continued to supply paper with the watermark C D G long after the death of Claude de George. The paper, however, was of excellent quality and not inferior (9) to that made during the lifetime of Claude de George.

The above picture is a reduced facsimile of a paper-wrapper in a collection of wrappers in the Municipal Archives at Amsterdam, and it is believed that the portrait, in cap and bells, is that of Abraham Janssen. The full names of the master paper-maker IM have not been discovered, but tracings of his watermarks — a foolscap and the arms of Amsterdam — appear in this work. In addition to Janssen's various watermarks his initials AI or *A J* always appear beneath the main watermark.

DURATION OF SOME OF THE CHIEF DUTCH WATERMARKS

	Traced from MSS. or Prints
Arms of Amsterdam	1635—1796
"VRYHEYT" in Wreath, Lion, spear and seven darts	1654—1720
"VRYHEYT" in crowned circle "Pro Patria ejusque Libertate"	1704—1810
Arms of the Seven Provinces, Lion, sword and seven darts in crowned shield	1656—1800
The same, "Eendraght maakt maght"	1667—1800
"Tuin", Garden of Holland, or Maid of Dort (Dordrecht) "PRO PATRIA"	1683—1799
Arms of Orange Nassau	1616—1767
Dutch Royal Rider	1762—1796
Dutch Royal Heads	1815—1840
Anglo-Dutch arms	1697—1741
The Beehive of Messrs. Honig	1683—1807
Arms of England	1733
Arms of London	1694
Britannia	1650
British Royal Monograms	1687—1775

IMITATION OF DUTCH WATERMARKS

The imitation of Dutch paper and watermarks by the French during the 18th century has been mentioned above. There was some excuse for this because the industry had fallen into decay, and the Dutch being the leading paper-makers and distributors, it was found necessary to follow their methods of manufacture. The same reason did not exist for German mills, which had been established far longer than those of Holland. (19) Nevertheless those of Württemberg and Bavaria imitated Dutch paper (17) and the trade marks of one of the leading firms. Specimens of imitated watermarks and descriptions of them are given here: —

The Kautenbacher Paper Mill in Bavaria was owned by the paper-makers Adolf, Louis and Richard Böcking.

This mill prided itself on its paper, which was used specially for official purposes. This paper had as watermark the coat-of-arms which

was copied from specimens of "Pro Patria" from the Dutch paper mill "At the sign of the Golden Beehive at Zaandyk". The pleasure which the enterprise gave to the brothers Böcking is borne out by a correspondence with the Zweibrüchen Revenue Office dated 18 March, 1790, which

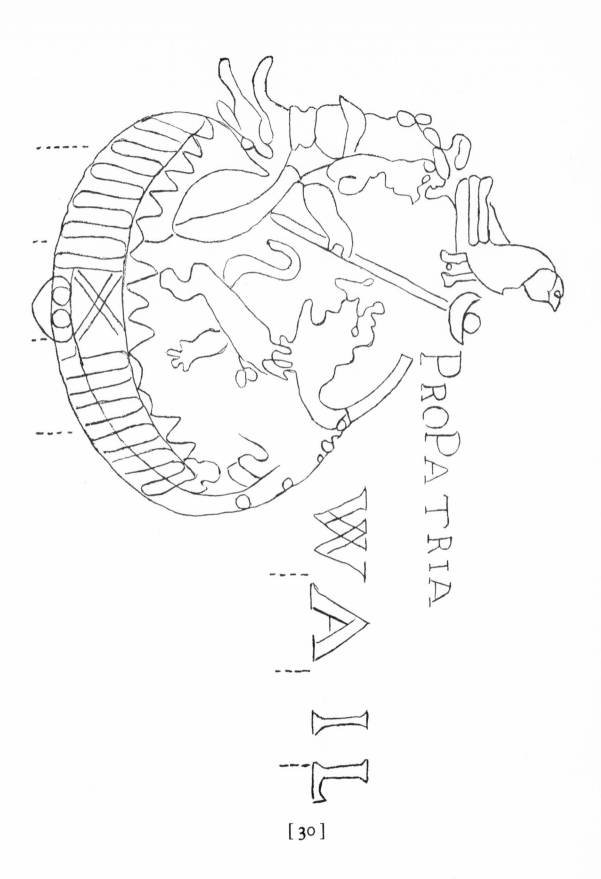

PRO PATRIA

WA IL

states that the coat-of-arms paper quoted at 4 gulden a ream was in great demand and used considerably more than the Dutch sorts of paper from the Golden Beehive quoted at 7 gulden a ream.

The mark shown on the opposite page of Johan Lorch of Wachtels-mühle in Bavaria, and the following is a description of the mark: —
(17) "Hollandiadarstellung, überhöht von Pro Patria-Devise und einem Vogel (Wachtel) als redendes Wappen der Wachtelsmühle im ersten Bogenblatt, die Buchstaben W A J L als Herstellermarke im zweiten Bogenblatt des 1798 beschriebenen Bogens".

A Swedish imitation is also given here. The Gransholm Paper Mill was founded at Gransholm in the South of Sweden in 1790. Each mark was in the centre of each half sheet.

VAN DER LEY

The above Pro Patria mark with the name Van der Ley is an imitation that was found on paper in Sweden. It shows several departures from the conventional design, and the printing is defective.

The following imitated mark was found also in Sweden The countermark was also VAN DER LEY: —

The following is a tracing of a mark made in Genoa. The initials are those of Giacomo Gambino, and the leg in a corner of the sheet is his personal mark in allusion to his surname: —

[33]

LIST OF REAM WRAPPERS OF PAPER

I. AT THE AMSTERDAM CITY ARCHIVES

Name	*Watermark*	*Mill*
Pierre Dexmier	Arms of Amsterdam	
Giles Dalidet	Foolscap	Angoumois
Maistre L. P.	Foolscap	Angoumois
Leoben Teenyere	Lily and lotus	
I. Salhan	French lily shaded	Périgord
Veuve Dexmier et F. De-clide	Amsterdam arms	Angoumois
Jean Rousselot (1630)	Foolscap	Angoumois
Jean Roulet (1638—61)	Ship, neptune, mermaid	Angoumois
Carrabin	Eagle, double headed, G V D on breast	
H. C. Wend & Zoonen	Garden of Holland	
Cornelis de Haes (1664)	Hare	Merchant of Amsterdam
Maistre Roulet		
A. Janssen		Angoulême
Jean Villedary	Amsterdam arms	Angoumois
Pierre Galtier (1648)	Crown, plain	Angoumois
I. H.	Arms of United Provinces	
L. V. G. (1741)	Arms of United Provinces	Egmond
P. L.	Amsterdam arms	
S. v. K. & W. (1745)	Garden of Holland, and crowned G. R.	
Estienne Planteau	Foolscap	Périgord
Adriaan Rogge (1776)	Vryheyt, and whale	Zaandam
Hendrik Raket (1751)	United Provinces Foolscap, 8 points	Zaandyk

"Les 7 Provinces Unies"	(1669)	
A. W.	Amsterdam arms	
A. L. W. & Co.	Garden of Holland	
Jean Villedary	Foolscap	Angoumois

Janssen "I. M."	Foolscap	Angoumois
G. G. à Montignac	Crowned crest "Fine, Superfine, Fine- paper"	Perigord
I. G.	Eagle, & "Timbre Im- perial"	Mill near Epinal
Jean Villedary for Francois van Tongeren	Amsterdam arms	Angoumois
Same	"Fine, Superfine, Fine- Paper" Amsterdam arms Amsterdam arms. "Papier fin Fait au Grand Moulin du Sieur de Beauvaix par Me. Pierre Bernard". Garden of Holland, Arms of Amsterdam within the garden. Above, in a crowned cartouche: "Les Sept Provinces Unies," and "Fine, Superfine, Fine Paper".	

II. REAM WRAPPERS IN THE AUTHOR'S COLLECTION

1710	Francois van Tongeren	Amsterdam arms	
1690	Pierre Riflaud	Amsterdam arms	
	Pierre Dexmier	Amsterdam	F. C. = Francois Chatonet?
1737	J. Kool	Amsterdam	
1744	I. V.	Amsterdam	
1782	I. Villedary	Amsterdam, and L. V. G.	
1670	Jean Villedary	Amsterdam, Angoumois	
		Amsterdam	
1808	Kloppenburg	Garden of Holland	

1796	I. V.		Garden of Holland
1790	I. H. & Z.	(Honig)	Garden of Holland
1752	C. & I. H.	(Honig)	Garden of Holland
	Van der Ley		Garden of Holland
	H. R.	(H. Raket)	Garden of Holland
1770	H. C. H.	(Hoysing)	Garden of Holland, lion alone
1749	L. V. G.	(Gerrevink)	Garden of Holland, lion alone
1795	D. & C. Blauw		Vryheyt
	F. & C.	(Forsten & Co.)	Vryheyt
	W. & C. Pannekoek		Vryheyt
1791 1802	Kloppenburg		Vryheyt
	C. & I. H.		Vryheyt
	Daniel Juilhard		Eendraght, plain Faugère mill in Périgord
	L. V. G.		Eendraght, plain
	C. & I. H.		Eendraght, plain
1754	I. H.		Eendraght, plain

(P. Dürring of Basle?)	
I. V. and L. V. G.	Lily, shaded
C. & I. H.	Lily, shaded
Hendrik Raket	Postilion
Adriaan Rogge	Postilion and whale
I. Honig & Zoonen	Postilion
C. & I. Honig	Postilion
D. & C. Blauw	Post horn
Van Gelder	Post horn

1802	Van der Ley	Post horn
	I. H.	Post horn
	C. & I. H.	Post horn
	J. Kool & Comp.	Post horn
	J. Kool	Tree, surmounted by cap of Liberty, and the word "LIEBERTE" beneath
	Jean Roulet	Le Got mill Angoumois
1671	Estienne Touzeau	Foolscap, between foolscap and legend
1808	H. Koldewyn	Garden of Holland
	I. V.	Garden of Holland, Guelderland coat-of-arms within and words: "Super fyn fyn" beneath
	I. V.	Garden of Holland Maid alone holding a palm
	D. & C. Blauw	Vryheyt
	Van Gelder	"Eendragt maakt magt"
1640 1670	C. D. H.(Cornelis de Haes)	"Op de hoek v/d Papenbrugh, Inde Papiermoolen tot Amsterdam"
	H. R. (H. Raket)	in shield, surmounted by tree.

There are three varieties of the Garden of Holland watermark, viz.
(1) maid alone in the garden; (2) maid and lion together, and (3) the
lion alone, like the tiger of Niger in the Limerick.

III. SOME OF THE REAM WRAPPERS IN THE COLLECTION OF MR. G. J. HONIG OF KOOG AAN DE ZAAN

| 1721 | Ieers Vierrevant | Garden of Holland Mill on the Zaan 7 Provinces |
| | C.D.G.(Claude de George) | Private coat-of-arms, and motto: "En vain espère qui ne craint Dieu" |

	H. K.	Garden of Holland	
	VE & FDE	Anchor in oval	(Veuve Dexmier et F. Declide?)
	T. R.	Garden of Holland	Rotterdam
1780	D. B.	Garden of Holland	Rotterdam
	D. I. Schut	Foolscap	Veluwe
	Gt. Hesselink		
	A. & I. H.	Garden of Holland	
	I. V. & L. V. G.		
	F. & C.	Lily, shaded	
	C. & I. Honig		
	Konig & Desjardyn		
	M. van Lier	Garden of Holland	
	W. Otterloo	Garden of Holland, and crowned G. R.	
	VAN DER LEY	Arms of England	
1734	VAN DER LEY	Windmill, with arms of Zaandyk on the mill and monogram of Pieter van der Ley	
	I. Honig & Zoon	Foolscap	
	I. Honig & Zoon	Arms of England, 2 varieties	
1774	I. Hummen	Vryheyt	
1668	*C*	Windmill, and beneath the legend: "D. Papr Moole"	

"Papier fait par Jacques Corneille Miel au moulin de la Ruche à Miel". This appears to be Jacob Cornelis Honig's little joke.

There are many more wrappers in this collection.

ENGLAND

The first European paper that was used in England came from Italy and France from the early 14th century until the end of the 16th century. During this period there were two English mills: that of John Tate at Stevenage in Herts 1494—98, and that of John Spielman at Dartford in Kent 1588—1605. Wynkyn de Worde printed on Tate's paper in the production of Bartholomaeus' "De Proprietatibus Rerum" and Caxton's translation of the "Legende Aurea" of Jacobus de Voragine. A rare, and perhaps unique combination consists of Caxton's Printer's device and Tate's (21) watermark on the same sheet. This curiosity is treasured in the office of the Paper Makers' Association of Great Britain. The following is an eye-copy of it:

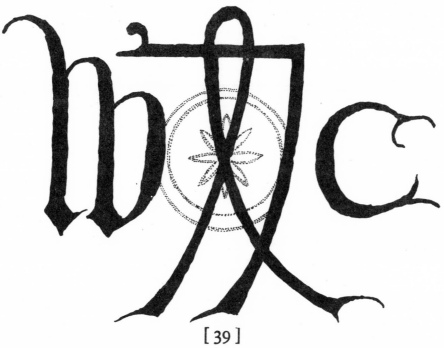

[39]

Swiss and German paper made its appearance in England during the latter part of the 16th century. At the beginning of the 17th century paper in use in England came from France, Switzerland, Germany and Italy. French paper came from Amsterdam, but mainly from Bordeaux and La Rochelle, and that from Switzerland and Germany from Amsterdam. Dutch paper began to enter England in appreciable quantities in the last (22) quarter of the 17th century. Until then French, Italian and Swiss paper continued to be imported, but during the 18th century most of the imports came from Holland, and were of Dutch manufacture. Several attempts were made to manufacture paper in England up to the beginning of the 18th century, but the mills were of short duration and unable to supply the national demand.

Fine white paper began to be made in this country on a fairly large scale in the second half of the 18th century, when James Whatman established (22/3) his famous mill at Maidstone. For a considerable time Whatman papers were made at two mills, at one in Kent and at another in Holland. The produce of one mill was distinguished by the watermark "J. Whatman, Turkey Mill", and the other "J. Whatman" accompanied by the initials L V G, the initials of L. van Gerrevink of Egmond a/d Hoef in North Holland. At this time Holland excelled in the art of papermaking, and it (23) is in that country that Whatman learnt the art. One may infer that he acquired his knowledge in the mill of Lubertus van Gerrevink, a celebrated manufacturer. Enquiries have been made in Holland in an endeavour to confirm this assumption, but without success. There have been many paper-makers of the same name in various parts of Holland, which increases the difficulty in tracing a particular one. There were two paper-makers with the same initials, at the same time and both in North Holland, whose mills were both named the Phoenix. It was probably for this reason that Lubertus van Gerrevink, the owner of the Egmond mill, had his initials registered as a trade-mark in 1726, to distinguish his paper from that made by Lucas van Gerrevink.

An even older established firm than that of J. Whatman is the firm of the Portals of Laverstoke mill in Hampshire. The Portals were Huguenots who fled from France during the persecutions that followed the revocation of the Edict of Nantes. Henry Portal, one of the survivors of the family who succeeded in escaping, came to England and was employed in a mill belonging to the Governor and Company of White Papermakers in England. In 1718 he acquired the Laverstoke mill, which the family has maintained to this day. Henry Portal died in 1747 and was succeeded by his son Joseph Portal, who managed the mill until his death in 1793, and his son John Portal continued the business until his death in 1848. The firm have been sole makers of bank-note paper for the Bank of (24) England since 1725.

Watermark No. 414 bears the name of J. Portal and the initials of Lubertus van Gerrevink. Watermark No. 413 bears the name of J. Bates and the same initials. With the firm of Whatman this makes three English firms connected with the same Dutch mill. Messrs. Portal were asked whether they could explain the connection between their firm and that of Gerrevink in the past, but they were unable to throw any light on the subject.

Besides the firms named above, the following names appear in watermarks on paper up to 1764: —

Elliston and Basket 1693; Heath 1743; Crowder 1745; Wickwar 1754; Curteis and Son 1763; Durham 1763; J. Nind 1764. These appear to be merchants or manufacturers with works abroad.

"The World's Paper Trade Review" of May 5, 1922 contains interesting information concerning old paper mills and hereditary owners. It is based on a humble 18 page pamphlet $4^1/_4''$ by $2^3/_4''$, and is a great contrast to the bulky papermakers' directories of the present day. This old directory is dated 1853 and belongs to the Paper Makers' Association in London.

Information concerning the industry in the 18th century is exceedingly scanty, because the archives belonging to the trade were destroyed by fire and cannot be replaced.

John Bagford, who lived between 1665 and 1715, collected a mass of material which he intended to incorporate in a work on Printing and Papermaking, but he did not live long enough to achieve his object. The material is in the British Museum among the Harleian MSS. numbered 5891—6988.

In 1690 the Paper Sellers appealed to Parliament to oppose the passage of a law to encourage the making of white paper in England on the ground that it would be a monopoly, that the makers could not supply

[41]

the English market, and that many people who live by the foreign paper industry, and the publishing trade, would lose their livelihood. The Governor and Company of White Papermakers stated that the Sellers were defending the interests of France, and that the English manufact-
(25) urers were brown paper makers.

Until 1690 England paid £ 100,000 annually for paper to France
(26) and Holland.

The Paper Sellers, who were monopolists, opposed the manufacture of white paper in England also because other sellers would buy from the national factories and not from the wholesale importers, whose trade accordingly would be seriously diminished. The monopolists were thus
(25) advocating Free Trade rather than Protection.

There were at the time seven monopolizing Paper Sellers in England. The Stationers joined in appealing to Parliament to obstruct the bill. At this juncture the French Ambassador intervened in support of the im-
(25) porters of French paper.

The word "COMPANY" has been found frequently as a water-mark on paper imported into England. The word may be intended for the East India Company, but more probably for the Company of White Papermakers mentioned above. The word being enclosed in a cartouche gives it the appearance of being a French watermark.

FOOLSCAP

In the beginning of the 17th C. writing paper was usually 12—13 inches in height and about 16 inches in width, folded in two, each half sheet measured about 12 by 8 inches. A common watermark on the paper was a jester in cap and bells. This was also the mark of John Spielman who began papermaking in 1588. The first edition of Shakespeare's plays printed by Isaac Jaggard and Ed. Blount in 1623 was said to have been printed on paper with this mark. The successors of this firm stated that the paper for Shakespeare's folios was imported from Holland. At that time the Dutch had not started the manufacture of fine white paper, but they traded in French, German and Swiss paper.

As usual when a monarchy is succeeded by a republic, royal emblems are destroyed or removed, and it is said that Cromwell ordered the royal arms watermark on official paper to be replaced by the figure of a fool in cap and bells. Careful search has been made in British archives in order to verify the allegation, but the specimens containing such a mark that have been found are extremely rare and of French origin. The mark was in existence one hundred years before the Commonwealth. On the other hand, several watermarks of hats have been found in various archives, and the shapes bore a strong resemblance to Puritans' hats. A specimen is given in Samuel Denne's observations on paper marks published in Archaeologia Vol. XII 1796. Referring to it he says: "A sheet for the year 1649 has for a device a large hat, and if an allusion to the fashion of the time was intended, it would denote the broad-brimmed beaver worn by the Puritans and republicans of that age." The mark lasted about thirty years.

The watermark was sought for as a guarantee of quality, and particular sizes of paper became known from their watermarks, such as Crown, Hand, Pot, Post, etc. Writing paper of the size given above became known in England as foolscap, and continues to bear that name. The foolscap watermark is no longer seen but has been replaced by Britannia or the Dutch lion. The only explanation why a Dutch watermark should appear on English paper is that the Dutch excelled in the manufacture of paper during the 18th Century and used their national emblem as a watermark. Much of this paper came to England, and English manufacturers had to imitate it in every detail when they determined to compete with Dutch manufacturers; they are so conservative that they are still making use of the Dutch lion on foolscap paper.

Although foolscap has meant a certain size of paper in England, it has not the same meaning on the Continent, where the mark is often found on writing paper, but has been found also on printing paper used by cartographers for engraving maps. W. Blaeu's maps of the 17th century were occasionally engraved on paper measuring 20″ by 23″ bearing a foolscap watermark.

BRITANNIA

One of the marks used to distinguish English foolscap size of paper is the Britannia watermark. It seems incredible that we had to go to Holland for our Britannia watermark, but it seems that this was the case. The British watermark appears to have been evolved from one of the Pro Patria watermarks representing the maid of Holland, seated within a palisade and holding a hat on the point of a spear (watermarks Nos. 127—153). The explanation of this picture is that Holland, surrounded by her fortified frontiers, maintains liberty by force of arms. The Pro Patria motto in the Britannia watermark No. 224 dated 1765 is manifestly Dutch. The English modification of this motto was "Pro Rege et Patria". The motto in the Britannia watermark No. 222 is decidedly foreign in its orthography.

POST PAPER

In England "post paper" is understood to mean a certain size, but on the Continent it meant formerly paper with the post horn watermark.

The horn watermark has lasted all down the centuries from the early part of the 14th century.

An early mention of post paper is contained in a Dutch Ordinance of 1636, which describes various sorts of paper and includes their origin and the duty per ream. In this Ordinance post paper is put down as of German origin.

In 1643 Cornelis de Haes, paper merchant of Amsterdam, imported paper from Bordeaux with the "Post-horn" watermark.

Bagford's collection of paper at the British Museum contains a wrapper of paper supplied by Paulus Sebelle, paper merchant of Amsterdam, whose watermarks were a horn in a shield, and a postilion blowing a horn. The following wording accompanied the marks: "Post papier te koop tot Amsterdam".

J. C. and A. van der Ley and J. Honig of Zaandyk had covers of reams of paper with pictures on them representing mounted postmen with letter pouch and horn. Both these firms made paper during the 18th and latter part of the 17th centuries with the horn watermark.

The above is Messrs. Van Gelder's wrapper mark for their Post paper.

PAPER MADE IN HOLLAND, FRANCE AND OTHER COUNTRIES FOR THE BRITISH MARKET, WITH BRITISH ROYAL CIPHERS AS COUNTERMARKS

(For meaning of abbreviations see p. 65)

Date of MS.	Countermark	Watermark	Locality of MS.
1687/8	Crowned GR	Dutch Lion	PRO K.William's Chest
1690	same	Pro Patria	PRO SP 32/3
1702	Crowned WR	Sword in wreath	PRO SP 34/1
1705	Crowned AR	Arms of Amsterdam	PRO SP 34/6
1706	Crowned GR	Arms of England	PRO SP 34/8
1707	Crowned AR	same	PRO CO 137/45
1708	Crowned GR	Arms of England	WCL D 688
1707	Crowned AR	Arms of England and Holland	PRO SP 34/9
1711	Crowned AR	Vryheyt	PRO CO 42/13
1720	Crowned GR	Genoese mark	EH
1720	same	Dutch Royal Rider	CC
1726	same	Arms of London	PRO CO 137/46
1733	same	Arms of England v/d Ley & Honig	CC
1740	GR & Bell	Pro Patria	PRO SP 36/50
1745	Crowned GR	J. Villedary	PRO SP 71/8
1762	same	Dutch Royal Rider	CC
1763	GR & Bell	Britannia, Pro Patria	WCL Accounts
1764	Crowned R & Bell	Britannia	WCL Accounts
1773	GR & Bell	Britannia	
1775	same	Horn in shield	WCL Accounts
1776	GR	same and LVG	WCL D 842
1780	Crowned GR	Dutch lion Pro Rege et Patria	PRO SP 37/14
1785	same	Vryheyt	CC
1799	same	J. Villedary	CC

The Hollanders were certainly quick to adapt themselves to changes of market requirements when they produced a crowned watermark for their King one year before his accession to the British throne. They varied the letters to suit Gulielmus or William, Anne and the Georges, but in some cases they put their own initials under the crown, or those of the consignees of their produce.

The above are some of the watermarks (reduced) of the firm of B. Cramer who have had mills in Holland since the year 1711.

ALPHABETICAL LIST OF BRITISH PAPER-MAKERS AND MILLS

Dates are those on MS. or print. Date in bold type, thus: **1794,** signifies paper dated by watermark. P. M. A. — Paper Makers' Association of Great Britain.

1845	Allford, R. & J. I.
1826	Alton mill
1835	Ansell
1837	Ansell, C.
1846—54	Ansell, C.
1812	Ansell, J.
1821	Atlee
1797	Apsley mill, Lily watermark
1809	Apsley mill bought by J. Dickinson
1800	Arnold & Foster Ld. Eynsford Mills, Kent
1853	Baldwin, James, mill No. 169
1808	Balston, W., and J. Whatman
1853	Balston & Co., mill No. 298, successors of J. Whatman
1783	Band & Son
1854	Barnard, R.
1817	Basted mill
1775	Bates, J.
1865 P.M.A.	Bates, J.
1836	Bevan & Co.
1853	Bishop & Blundell, London mill
1800 P.M.A.	Blackwell, A., Apsley mill
1801	Blackwell, A., and G. Jones, Apsley mill
1825	Booth
1803	Botfield
1807	Botfield, T. W. & R.
1824	Bridge mill
1815	Brookman & Skeats
1818	Brown, John
1818	Budgen, J.
1853	Burt, William

1780	**1809**	Buttanshaw
1801		Buttw, I.
1780		Buttanshaw, J.
1846		C. & Ansell
1829		Canson. Mill No. 370. There was a Canson of the Annonay paper mills of France in 1796
1804		Chandler, W. & T.
1853		Christopher. Southwark mill, London
1851		Clarke & Co.
1821		Clarke & Horsington
1822		Coles, Joseph
1799—48		Coles, J.
1853		Cooper & Phillips, London
1805		Corbett, J.
1817		Cottuams mill
1800		Cowan, Charles. St. Mary Cray mill, Kent
1825		Craft, G.
1805		Cripps, J.
1800		Crispe & Newman
1853		Cropper, James, mills Nos. 162, 165
1745		Crowder
1763		Curteis & Sons
1831		Davis
1853		Davis, Richard. Bermondsey mill, London
1811		De Montairt mill, Bath
before 1850		Dewdney, John, of Devon
1814		Dickinson, John, & Co., Apsley mill. (PRO SP 16/521)
1818		Dobbs
1853		Dunster, Thomas, London
1764—90		Durham
1801		Durham, W.
1785		Durham & Co.
1796		Dusautoy, J. A.
1807		Dusautoy & Rump

[49]

1801	Edmonds & Pine
1814—47	Edmonds, T.
1697 1778	Eliston & Basket
1846	Emberlin
1844	Evans, S., & Co.
1778	E. & S.
1837	Fellows
1810	Fellows, John
1821	Fellows & Sons
1823	Fincher & Sons
1780	French, T., with Dutch watermarks
1770	Garnett, P. W.
1801	Gater
1815	Gater, J.
1837	Gater, J. & E.
1822	Gilling & Alford
1798	Golding & Snelgrove
1853	Goodall, J. C., Camden Town mill, London
1788	Greaves of Warrington
1810	Green, J. Barcham, - & Son, mill No. 310, Maidstone
1831	Green, G. H.
1815	Green, J.
1690	Grosvenor & Chater, Abbey mills, Holywell, N. Wales First Stationers to the Bank of England
1821	Hagar & Co.
1800	Hale, C.
1829	Hall, John
1839	Hall
1844	Hall, W.
1821	Harrison, J.
1853	Hart & Son, London
1853	Hatcher, St. Luke's, London
1853	Hatchett, Spitalfields, London
1832	Harris & Tremlett

1824	Heale mill
1743	Heath
1853	Hodgkinson, mill No. 366
1802	Holland & Co.
1780—1800	Holyoak, J.
1853	Hunt & Sons of London
1853	Jackson, John, mill No. 163
1844	James, Thomas, Hurcott mill
1853	Jefferis, John, Stepney mill, London
1853	Jefferis & Co.
1821	Jones, E.
1804	Jones, G.
1848	Joynson mill No. 327, Kent { Wm. Joynson & Son, St. Mary Cray, Kent is still Mill 327
1818	Key Brothers & Son
1780—1850	King, W., with Dutch watermark
1808	Kingsford, W.
1800	Koops, Matthias, Neckinger mill, Bermondsey, London
1840	Langley & Stevens
1853	Lamb, John, mill No. 491
1780—1801	Lay, S.
1832	Leek, J. A.
1794	Lepard, William
1805	Lloyd, J.
1798	Lloyd & Co.
1809	Ludlow
1791	Matlock
1822	Middleton & Hodgkinsons
1834	Mills, H.
1830	Mills, J. M.
1832	Minter, John
1860	Monier
1837	Morbey

1824	Mum & Stephen
1818	Munn, G. R.
1780—1814	Munn, L.
1838	Munn, R., & Co. Kent mill
1853	Nash, M. A., mill No. 587
1853	Nash, William
1850	Nash
1807	Nash mill, bought by J. Dickinson & Co.
1808	Newton, N.
1764—1797	Nind, J. probably a merchant at first importing from Holland, and manufacturer in 1797
1777	O. & C.
1800	Olive & Parkington
1825	P. G.
1810	Paine, Edward
1794	Patch, C.
1825	Phair, W.
1812	Phipps & Son
1814	Pickering, W., & Co.
1800	Pike, C.
1810	Pine & Thomas
1780	Portal, J., Laverstoke mill
1796	Portal & Co.
1853	Portal, W. S., mill No. 337. Makers of bank-notes to the Bank of England
1796	Post, Tk.
1812	Radway
1807	Redway
1853	Reynolds J., & Son, London
1853	Roberts, William, London
1838	Romsey mill
1832	Rowland
1820	Rump, J.
1800	Ruse

1805—45	Ruse & Turner
1797	Russell & Co.
c 1775	S., countermark L V G
1853	Sabine H. R., Fleet Street mill, London
1848	Saunders, I. H.
1843	Sellers, W.
1810	Sharp, W.
1814	Sharp, W. & S.
1802	Skeats
1822	Slade
1798	Smith
1816—54	Smith & Alnutt
1814	Smith, E.
1843	Smith, I. & I.
1853	Smithson & Mayfield, mill No. 153
1807—28	Snelgrove
1833	Snelgrove, M.
1823	Snelgrove & Son
1798	Stace, A.
1795	Stevens, J.
c 1770	Stirling, R. W.
1849	Stradling, W.
1828	Sweetapple
1784	S. & W.
1768—90	Taylor, C.
1777—95	Taylor & Co.
1853	Taylor, John
1853	Taylor Sr., John
1853	Taylor Jr., John
1746—94	Taylor, I.
1824	Thomas, W.
1853	Towgood, Alfred., mill No. 296
1851	Towgood
1838	Town, J. & J.

1853	Tremlett, E. N. mill No. 94
1815	Tucker, W.
	Tullis, Russell & Co. mill No. 10, Edinburgh
1853	Turnbull, J.
1853	Turnbull, J. L. & J. mill in Finsbury, London
1824	Turner, G. & R.
1822	Turner, R., & Son
1802	Turner, W.
1806—45	Turner & Turner
1835	Venables, E. I., & Co.
1679	Ward, James, of London. Importer of paper from the Honigs, Holland
1844	Warren, W.
1713	Watkin, Thomas
1819—40	Weatherley
1765 to date	Welles & Grosvenor
1760—1850	Whatman, James., Turkey mill, Kent
1754—80	Wickwar
1780—94	Wickwar, J.
1801	Wilding, E.
1776—89	Williams, R.
1794	Wilmott
1798—1821	Wilmott, C.
1836—89	Wilmott, G.
1804	Wise, John
1847	Wise & Stacy

FRANCE

There seems to be as much uncertainty concerning the origin of papermaking in France as in Italy. Some trace the origin to French Crusaders, who are said to have learnt the art while prisoners of the Saracens in Syria.

The water-wheel or Catherine wheel watermarks given below are symbolical of the Crusader legend. They are copies of Briquet's Nos. 13322/3, and the MSS. from which they were traced are dated 1469/72, nearly. (13) two centuries after the last Crusade. Others, with more probability, trace

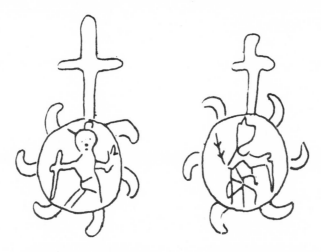

the beginnings to Spain, where the art was introduced by the Arabs in the middle of the 12th century. What is beyond doubt, however, is that trade in paper was carried on by the Lombards at the fairs held at Troyes from the beginning of the 14th century. For a time these travelling Italian merchants enjoyed an absolute monopoly, and took advantage of it to raise their prices. These became so excessive that the King of France granted letters

[55]

patent to the University of Paris in 1354, giving it the right to select four sworn paper-makers at Troyes and Essonne, in the province of Champagne, who should make fine paper for the use of the University, in return for which the manufacturers would be exempt from any kind of taxation. (15) The University continued to employ sworn paper-makers throughout the 17th and 18th centuries.

The following watermarks were used by sworn paper-makers. According to Briquet a mark like the one on the left was used by the Nivelles from 1511 to nearly the end of the 16th century.

Another watermark used by sworn paper-makers was a bell with the word JURÉ. The shape of the bell is like the coat-of-arms of the University of Paris reversed, the quatrefoil or rose of Troyes forming the clapper of the bell. The bell watermark was a French guarantee of fine quality and was eventually adopted in Holland and England, possibly for the same purpose.

The vocabulary of the French paper-makers' industry is partly derived from the Italian. This circumstance and the fact that Colbert enticed Italian workmen to come to France is conclusive evidence that Italian industry had a great influence on the development of French (27) paper industry.

[56]

When the paper industry of France had reached the importance of that of Italy, it was found necessary to protect it, and to prevent other nations from recruiting French workmen with the object of discovering the secrets of the trade. In order to maintain the supremacy of France in the industry, Colbert took drastic measures to prevent the emigration of French subjects. A decree of 1667 rendered emigrants liable to imprisonment and confiscation of property. And in 1682 the death penalty was imposed. The persecution of the Huguenots that followed the revocation of the Edict of Nantes compelled many of the paper-makers and their workmen, who were protestants, to seek refuge in the neighbouring countries, namely: Genoa, Spain, Germany, Switzerland, Holland and England. From 1685 the French industry declined for a time, and that of the neighbouring countries named profited by the immigration of skilled (27) French refugees.

A report to the Intendant of Auvergne stated that the art of paper-making in France flourished and made the greatest progress while left to itself during four centuries. During this time France supplied paper to several countries. The industry declined, however, in the middle of the 18th century in consequence of heavy taxation and vexatious regulations. On the other hand, the invention of the "Hollander" gave the Dutch a (13) great advantage over their French rivals.

In this connection an incident is related that occurred to a paper-maker in Auvergne. The man had gone to the nearest village on business, and on coming out of the inn, after having refreshed himself heartily, tried in vain to mount his mule. He then dropped on his knees and begged the Patron Saint of the local paper-makers to help him, saying: "Buon San Damian, juda me", Good St. Damian, help me. With the assistance of the good saint he made another effort, and this time he vaulted clear over the animal's back, and fell heavily to the ground. The disappointed man only remarked that the saint had helped too much. So it is with States (13) when they meddle with trade and industry, they do more harm than good.

The Law of 1688 regulating the manufacture of paper ordered that the initials of the surname and christian name of a paper-maker should be added to the watermark on every sheet of paper. Thus, Jean Villedary would have to add the letters I V on every sheet of paper made by him.

The Law of 1739/41 regulated the size and weight of all kinds of

[57]

paper according to their watermarks, and includes the arms of Amsterdam, Pro Patria, the 3 O's or 3 circles, and the arms of Genoa. It also mentions Spanish and Lombard types of paper. A regulation of 1739 is concerned with the export of paper to the Levant. The different sorts are named (9) three crescents or three moons (Venetian style). These regulations show that the French adopted well-known foreign marks for the export trade.

The tariff of 1741 that was attached to the Law of 1739 ordered that the year of manufacture must be shown in watermark, and that from the following 1st of January all paper should be marked 1742. The wording was not clear, and the result was that many papermakers marked their paper 1742 even until the end of the century. Accordingly French paper with 1742 in watermark is not always a guarantee that the paper was made in that year. For instance, an Ordinance that was printed in Amsterdam in 1768 concerning "Argent hachée" has the following watermark: Arms of Amsterdam, "J. Jardel fin Perigord 1742". The date 1742 in this case is of no use to confirm whether the Ordinance was an original or a reprint. But it is useful when prints purport to have been published earlier than the watermarked date. For example: "Antiquités d'Arles" is dated 1687, whereas the paper on which it is printed bears the watermark: "À Orange, Dauphiné, fin, 1742". Again, a History of England published at Amsterdam in 1730, bears the watermark: Arms of Amsterdam, "R. Jardel, fin, Perigord, 1742". Both these dates 1742 are clear evidence that the works described above are reprints.

From the 14th century onwards much of the paper used in England came from France, common watermarks being pot, hand and crown. In 1685 France exported paper to England, Spain, Switzerland, Denmark, Sweden, Russia and Holland. The twelve mills of Alsace exported 4000 bales, two (14) thirds of which went to Switzerland and Germany.

Fifty-six varieties of paper were made in France during the 18th century at the following centres:

AUVERGNE   There were fifteen mills at Thiers and fifty at Ambert. Thiers was famous for superfine writing paper and Ambert for printing paper.

ANGOUMOIS produced the finest qualities, mostly for export via Bordeaux and La Rochelle. According to De Lalande there were 400 mills in this district in the 17th century.

PÉRIGORD	produced the finest qualities like the above.
LIMOGES	produced good qualities for printing and engraving.
GUYENNE	,, ,, ,, ,, ,, ,, ,,
POITOU	,, ,, ,, ,, ,, ,, ,,
BRITTANY	produced ordinary qualities.
NORMANDY	Wrapping and coloured paper.
MAINE	Paper with hand and pot watermarks.
ETAMPES	,, ,, ,, ,, ,, ,,
CHAMPAGNE	Strong ordinary paper for printing and writing.
DAUPHINÉ	Superfine qualities.
PROVENCE	,, ,,
(29) VIVARAIS	All kinds of fine paper at Annonay.

Shortly before the Revolution there were fifty mills near Morlaix in Brittany, which produced 109,000 reams per annum, of which 2700 reams were consumed locally, and the rest was exported to Portugal and Holland, to the former for wrapping fruit and to the latter for printing.

(30)   At one of these mills at Quimperlé, a paper-maker named Georget made stamped paper (papier timbré) which was used by State functionaries. The watermark represents an eagle with the words "Timbre Im-
(30) perial" and the letter G. A specimen of the mark is given in this work under no. 546.

The paper mills of Brittany date from the 15th century. The industry was important at the beginning of the 17th century, and exported most of its produce to England via Morlaix. In 1729 the export to Holland, Spain and Portugal was reduced considerably in consequence of careless workmanship and dishonesty of the shippers. In 1756 the States of Brittany offered a reward for the best imitation of Dutch or Genoese paper. At this time Spain bought much paper from Holland and Genoa for re-export to their Possessions, and the French endeavoured to capture some
(30) of this important trade.

Examination of paper in the archives of a monastery at Santiago di Compostella, Spain, show that French paper found its way to Spain in the 18th century. Paper with the following marks has been found:

Arms of Amsterdam "J. Jardel" 1734
same   "J. Dumas, Périgord" 1763/72
same   "R. Jardel, Périgord 1742"

same	"D. Perie, Périgord"
same	"F. Marot, Périgord 1742"
Arms of Holland	"J. Villedary, for Gilis van Hoven"
	"Malrusie, Périgord 1742"
	"C. E. Blanchard EN MARCHE 1742"
Arms of Amsterdam	I ♡ S 18th century.
Arms of Genoa	"R. Jardel, Périgord 1742"
same	"I. Abadie, Bearn 1762"
same	"D. P. Monie, Bicorre 1766"
Three circles	"M. Racuette, Bearn 1770"

In 1789 there were sixty mills in Auvergne, but in the year II of the Republic the number had dropped to thirty-three. One of the leading firms to cease work was that of the Richards, who had been established for more than two centuries. The last of this long line of paper-makers was riding to a neighbouring town on business and on the road met one of his former workmen, who asked for a lift. This was granted, but the workman stabbed his former employer and appropriated his horse and the contents of his pockets. Some of the last paper made by the murdered paper-maker exists in the French edition of Capt. Cook's voyages published in 1785. The watermark reads: "FIN DE T ♡ RICHARD, AUVERGNE" which signifies not only (13) fine paper manufactured by T. Richard, but the tragic end of a famous and old-established firm.

SOME FAMOUS PAPER-MAKERS OF AUVERGNE:

1634	Johannot, formerly of Ambert, now at Annonay
1634	Mongolfier, formerly of Ambert, since at Vidalon
1634	La Roche Joubert, ,, ,, ,, ,, ,, Angoulême
1694	Nourisson, ,, ,, ,, ,, ,, Montargis, Orleanais
17th C.	Richards ,, ,, Auvergne
17th C.	Vimals ,, ,, ,,
1731	Sauvade ,, ,, Combe Basse mill. 1st edition of Moliére's works printed on their paper.

1751	T. Dupuy, Grand Rive mill. Manufacturers for the Royal Press. Their "Grand Raisin" for printing and writing was the finest produce of France.		
1731	Philibert Cusson	of Thiers	
1731	Riberolles Aîné	,,	,,
1731	J. Chabrier	,,	,,
1731	J. Nourisson	,,	,,
1731	Malmenayde	,,	,,
1789	Pierre Balland	,,	,,
1789	Pierre Balland Aîné	,,	,,
1789	Begon, Maignet, Micolon, Pourrat, Sauvade, Dupuy		
1717	Colombier of Ambert		
(13) 1717	Gourbeyre of Ambert		

The first treatise that was published in France on the art of paper-making was written by Father Imberdis in 1693. The writer was a Jesuit and native of Ambert in Auvergne, who lived among paper mills, and from his detailed description was quite familiar with the industry. After giving a most minute description of all the processes, he adds, as if afraid to have said too much, that what he has said is no secret in Holland or England, and that paper is far from perfect when it is released from the mould, but requires a thousand manipulations, and must pass through numerous hands before it becomes the finished article. Heaven, he says, does not allow a divine art to be made easy for mortals here below.

The writer gave two hints how to test writing paper. The first is to see how it reacts when being crumpled in the hands, and if the crumpling sounds like that of parchment, as it should when satisfactory. The second is to wet a piece of paper with the tongue, and if the saliva penetrates to any part of it, it will not be fit for manuscript.

Father Imberdis ends his descriptive poem by saying that if one requires further particulars one should come to Ambert, where 300 mills exist in the neighbourhood. Being an Auvergnat — a folk given to (31) exaggeration — one need not accept this number as absolutely correct.

The virtue of the paper industry has been extolled in various languages, and the following are some examples: —

At the end of Bartholomaeus' "De Proprietatibus Rerum" an epilogue in 13 stanzas has been added, and the following stanza refers to the paper industry:

"And also of your charyte call to remembrance
The soul of William Caxton, first prȳter of this boke
In laten tongue at Coleyn hȳself to avauce
That every well disposed man may thereon loke
And John Tate the yonger, Joye mote he broke,
Wich late hath in England doo make this paper thinne
That now in our English this boke is printed inne".

(Printed at Westminster by Wynkyn de Worde, 1496)

In the second part of Henry VI, Act IV, vij, Shakespeare makes Jack Cade, the rebel communist, accuse Lord Say of building a paper mill.

"A description and playne Discourse of Paper, setting foorth in verse a Paper-Myll built near Dartford, by a High Germaine, called Master Spilman, Jeweller to the Queenes Majesty, by Thomas Churchyard, 1588."

Extracts (modernized):

I praise the man that first did Paper make,
The only thing that sets all virtues forth:
It shows new books, and keeps old works awake,
Much more of price than all the world is worth:

If paper be so precious and so pure,
So fit for man and serves so many ways,
So good for use, and will so well endure,
So rare a thing, and is so much in praise:
Then he that made for us a Paper-mill,
Is worthy well of love and world's good-will.
And though his name be Spil-man by degree,
Yet Help-man, now, he shall be called by me".

[62]

Der Papyrer.

Ich brauch Hadern zu meiner Mül
Dran treibt mirs Rad deß waffers viel/
Daß mir die zſchnitn Hadern nelt/
Das zeug wirt in waffer einquelt/
Drauß mach ich Pogn/auff dē filtz bring/
Durch preß das waffer darauß zwing.
Denn henck ichs auff/laß drucken wern/
Schneweiß vnd glatt/ſo hat mans gern.

THE PAPER-MAKER

The water turns my mill wheel round,
Where rags to paper pulp are ground:
Their snowy leaves on felt I lay,
And squeeze the water well away,
And then I hang my sheets to dry:
All white, and shining like the sky.

Lines by the Meistersinger, Hans Sachs, about 1550. Engraving by
Jost Amman.

[63]

Uit afgesleeten linnendoeken,
Hier op te koopen, daar te zoeken:
Gewaschen en tot pap gebrugt,
Verschijnt papier, zoo waardgeacht.

THE PAPER-MAKER

White linen that is torn to rags,
Bought up and carried here in bags,
Is washed and then to pulp is made,
Then changed to paper of high grade.

Etching by Jan Luyken, published at Haarlem, 1695.

[64]

> "Le sage écrit sur parchemin,
> Sur coquille l'amant griffonne;
> L'excellence use du vélin,
> Et les rois ont pris la couronne,
> Sur tellière on lance un plan,
> Lise, pour tracer quelques lignes,
> Achéte du petit poulet."

Lines by Louis Festeau, in "Papeterie et Papetiers de l'ancien temps".

The following words used to be sung by contented companions at their work in a paper mill in the 18th century and was brought to light by Henri Pourrat in his delightful book, "Dans l'herbe des trois vallées":

> "Si le roi savait
> La vie que nous menons
> Quitterait son palais,
> Se ferait compagnon."

Of the virtue that springs from foul rags Voltaire said: —

> "Un ramas de guenilles et de sales chiffons
> Éternisent l'esprit des Plynes et d'un Buffon."

PARTICULARS CONCERNING WATERMARKS

Abbreviations:

CC	Mr. Churchill's collection of MSS., Prints and blank paper.
EH	Mr. E. Heawood's watermarks
PRO	Public Record Office
WCL	Worcester Cathedral Library
SAP	State Archives at Palermo
w/m	Watermark
c/m	Countermark
=	c/m belongs to w/m
ND	No date
SP	State Papers
CO	Colonial Documents
D	Documents

[65]

ARMS OF AMSTERDAM

1	1635	MS.	CC	This is a w/m of "I M" who is described as the master paper-maker who worked at the Puy-moyen mill for Sieur Janssen
2	1651		CC	
3	1654–85		CC	
4	1659		CC	
5	1662		CC	
6	1654–79		CC	C/m of Pierre Dexmier?
7	1662	Print	CC	
8	1665	MS.	CC	
9	1665	MS.	CC	W/m of C. van Gangelt and G. Bernard
10	1669	MS.	CC	
11	1670		CC	W/m of François Chatonet?
12	1671	MS.	CC	
13	1675		CC	W/m of Pieter v/d Ley. Specimen presented by Messrs. Van Gelder Zonen.
14	1672	MS.	CC	C/m M P
15	1679	MS.	CC	C/ms P D and V G
16	1678			Extract from a document of the city of Nymegen. Paper Makers' Association, London
17	1681			Late troubles in England, W. Dugdale
18	1682	Print	CC	W/m of Adriaan Cornelis and Jan Honig
19	1684	Print	CC	
20 & 21		Print	CC	
22	1686	Print	CC	
23	1686		EH	Chardin's Travels, London
24	1686		CC	
25	1690	MS.	CC	
26	1688		EH	Dapper's Archipelago, Amsterdam
27	1691		CC	Monogram of Gilis van Hoven, Dutch factor in Angoumois

28	1691	MS.	CC	
29	1693		CC	C/m L V G, initials of Lubertus van Gerre-vink
30	1692	MS.	CC	
31	1696	MS.	CC	and 1719
32	1693	MS.	CC	
33	1697	MS.	CC	
34	1698	MS.	CC	
35	1698		CC	End paper
36	1705		CC	
37	1700	MS.	CC	
38	1700	MS.	CC	
39	1703	MS.	CC	
40	1703		CC	
41	1706	MS.	CC	
42	1715	MS.	CC	Same w/m as No. 41, but with Beauvais instead of J. Villedary
43	1708	MS.	CC	
44	1781	MS.	CC	
45	1710	MS.	CC	
46	1711		CC	Same w/m with c/m I V dated 1707
47	1713	MS.	CC	
48	1720	MS.	CC	Beehive design under arms of Amsterdam indicates a Honig mill
49	XVIII C	MS.	CC	From St. Martin's Monastery Library, Santiago di Compostella, probably imitation mark from the South of France
50	1729	MS.	CC	
51	1734	MS.	CC	
52	1736		CC	The name I. Villedary & the initials L V G are frequently found on the same sheet. It is not known whether they worked together. Both were famous paper-makers, and it is not clear why both names appear

together unless as a double guarantee of excellence

53	1736	Print	CC	
54	1742		CC	C/m I W should perhaps be W I as in No. 16
55	1747	Print	CC	
56	1768		CC	
57	1787		CC	
58	1796	MS.		Van Gelder Zonen
59	1711	MS.	CC	Same w/m as that of Villedary, No. 41
60	1702	MS.	CC	Same w/m as that of P. Joly, No. 37, I S is possibly c/m of Jacques Salmon
61	1706	MS.	CC	Same w/m as that of P. v/d Ley, No. 13
62	1710	MS.	CC	Same w/m as that of P. Joly, No. 37
63	1721	MS.	CC	Same w/m as that of LMAU, No. 50
64	1795		CC	
65	ND		CC	
66	1808	Print	CC	
67	ND	MS.	CC	
68	ND		CC	
69	ND		CC	
70	ND		CC	Probably Genoese imitation
71	1768		CC	Crosses of unusual shape
72	1780	Print	CC	One cross instead of three
73	1787	Print	CC	Two crosses instead of three
74	1788	Print	CC	One Latin cross instead of 3 of St. Andrew
75	ND		CC	This mark has a star instead of 3 crosses Nos. 1 & 2, and 2 & 3 in centre of each half sheet
76	1695		EH	Thesaurus Geogr., London
77	1702	Print	CC	grotesque imitations of arms of Amsterdam
78	1781	Print	CC	

VRYHEYT

79	1720	MS.	CC	
80	1654	MS.	CC	W/m of J. Salmon?
81	1704		CC	W/m & c/m in centre of each half sheet and monogram in centre of the paper
82	1740	MS.	CC	
83	1745	PRO		SP 36/80 f 131, Crowder's Liberty. Crowder may have been an English paper-maker, but more probably an importer
84	1746		CC	
85	1750		CC	K in the centre of the paper stands for Jan Kool. The w/m is in the centre of the right half-sheet, and the c/m is in the centre of the left half-sheet
86	1757		CC	
87	ND		CC	
88	1762	PRO		CO 42/13 Possibly first English w/m of the kind
89	1769		EH	Tirion's Atlas, Amsterdam
90	1772		CC	
91	1770			"Strasburg Archives" by Paul Heitz, No. 352 c/m J. Pasquay of Alsace
92	1765	WCL		D 146/221 The w/m and motto Pro Rege et Patria seems to be an English variation of a Dutch mark
93	1779	PRO		SP 37/14 This is presumably the w/m and c/m of Joseph Portal, one of the oldest established paper-makers in England
94	1783		CC	W/m of Marten Schouten & Co.
95	1785		CC	Monogram of Adriaan Rogge
96	1799		CC	
97	1800	MS.	CC	Imitation found in Sweden, inferior paper
98	1808		CC	
99	1810		CC	

[69]

100	1813		CC	W/m of G. I. Brouwer
101	1813	MS.	CC	
102	ND		CC	W/m of Koning & Desjardyn
103	ND		CC	
104	ND		CC	
105	ND		CC	W/m and c/m in the centre of each foolscap sheet, and "3" between them
106	ND	CC		
107	1813	CC		W/m of Messrs J. Dickinson & Co., who presented paper with this mark to the writer. Isaia Thomas of Worcester, Mass. adopted this w/m in 1786. "Papermaking through Eighteen Centuries" by Dard Hunter, New York, 1930 p. 330
108	1913	CC		W/m of Messrs Alexander Cowan & Son. English foolscap paper bore this w/m as well as the Britannia mark, and was used extensively by Government Departments

SEVEN PROVINCES

109	1656	MS.	CC	C/m of Gilis van Hoven
110	1654	MS.	CC	W/m & c/m of Abraham Janssen and Claude de George
111	1669–1755	MSS.	CC	probably w/m of Villedary for Dirk and Ysbram Janssen
112	1672		EH	Baldecus, Amsterdam. May be WI, see No. 16
113	1675	MS.	CC	W/m and monogram of Pieter v/d Ley
114	1675	MS.	CC	
115	1698		CC	W/m of Lubertus van Gerrevink
116	1701	MS.	CC	W/m of A. Janssen and c/m of François Jardel
117	1707		CC	W/m of Jean Villedary

118	1707	MS.	CC	W/m of A. Janssen, and c/m of Claude de George
119	1777		CC	Voyages of Capt. Cook, by G. Foster, London
120	ND		CC	
121	ND	Print	CC	W/m of Koning & Desjardyn
122	ND		CC	

EENDRACHT

123	1667		CC	Grey blotting paper
124	ND		CC	W/m of Van der Ley
125	ND		CC	
126	ND		CC	

"TUIN", GARDEN OF HOLLAND, OR MAID OF DORT (DORDRECHT)

127	1683		CC	W/m and c/m of Abraham Janssen
128	1696		EH	Thevenot's collection of Travels, Paris
129	1701	MS.	CC	W/m of A. Janssen
130	1703		CC	W/m of Jan v/d Ley. Presented by Messrs. Van Gelder Zonen
131	1710	MS.	CC	
132	1711			W/ms of B. Cramer. The firm still exists
133	1713		CC	W/m of J. Villedary
134	1732	MS.	CC	Book of English legal forms, by G. Bishop
135	1755		CC	W/m of Pieter v/d Ley
136	1754	MS.	CC	
137	1769	MS.	CC	NP may be the initials of Nicolaas Panne-koek
138	1760		CC	W/m of J. Villedary. The legend "Pour l'Angleterre" shows that paper with this w/m was intended for the English market

139	1763		CC	Dutch Brewers' Regulations
140	1764		WCL	Accounts Lib XXXIV
141	1770	MS.	CC	
142	1772		EH	W/m of James Whatman?
143	1780		PRO	SP 37/14
144	1781		EH	Croydon Parish document
145	1783		EH	
146	1787		EH	
147	1795	MS.	CC	
148	1795		WCL	D 897. Probably first English imitation of this w/m
149	ND		CC	Thin blue unsized paper
150	1799	MS.	CC	
151	1799	MS.	CC	
152	ND		CC	
153	ND		CC	After 1742

ARMS OF ORANGE NASSAU

154	1616	EH	End paper in Frankfort book
155	1753	CC	W/m of J. Villedary or J. Vierrevant
156	1767	CC	
157	1775	CC	

LIONS (CONCORDIA, ETC.)

158	ND	CC	W/m of Van der Ley
159	ND	CC	
160	ND	CC	Print
161	ND	CC	Print
162	ND	CC	W/m of Van der Ley, "God zij met ons"

ANGLO-DUTCH COATS-OF-ARMS

163	1697		Dict. des Filigranes, F. Del Marmol, Brussels
164	1741	CC	
165	ND	CC	Middle XVIII C

DUTCH ROYALTIES

166	1762	CC	
167	1771	CC	
168	1772	CC	
169	1780	CC	
170	1790	CC	
171	1796	CC	
172	1815	CC	Name between the two w/ms
173	1815	CC	W/m of Jan Honig & Zoon
174	1815	CC	C/m of No. 173
175	1815	CC	

DUTCH PROVINCES AND CITIES

176	1673		CC	Arms of Zaandyk, GP = Gerrit Pietersz, w/m of Pieter v/d Ley. Paper presented to the writer by Messrs Van Gelder Zonen
177	1755	Print.	CC	Arms of Groningen
178	1835		CC	Arms of Middelburg and Zeeland, w/m of S. van Benthem. Both in centre of each half of sheet

BEEHIVE

179	1683–1902	CC	
180	1683	CC	W/m of J. Honig & Zoon
181	1798?	EH	Boccage papers, Paris

[73]

182	1825?		EH	Natural History of Birds, Amsterdam
183	ND	MS	CC	Apparently a foreign imitation
184	ND		CC	
185	ND		CC	

ELEPHANT

186	1663		Map engraved in Amsterdam. Scots' House, Veere
187	XVII C	CC	
188	1630	CC	
189	1786	CC	Map engraved in Amsterdam, w/m of Adriaan Rogge
190	ND	CC	W/m of N. Pannekoek after 1717
191	1800	CC	

MISCELLANEOUS MILL MARKS

192	1740	CC	
193	XVIII C	CC	W/m of Van der Ley
194	ND	CC	W/m of D. & C. Blauw
195	ND	CC	
196	ND	CC	W/m of Jan Kool
197	1800	CC	Map engraved in Amsterdam, size 83 × 67 cm.
198	1821	CC	Map engraved in Amsterdam, name alone in w/m
199	1799	CC	W/m of Pieter v/d Vries & Co.
200	1808	CC	
201	ND	CC	

WRAPPERS OR LABELS FOR REAMS OF PAPER

202	1720	CC	Arms of Amsterdam, picture of Guelderland paper mill between the supporters. Name of maker is unknown
203	ND	CC	W/m of Lubertus van Gerrevink and J. Villedary
204	ND	CC	W/m of Forsten & Co.
205	ND	CC	W/m of J. Villedary
206	ND	CC	W/m of J. Villedary
207	ND	CC	
208	ND	CC	
209	ND	CC	Contemporaneous with French Revolution

ARMS OF ENGLAND

210	1637	EH	Camden's Britannia. This w/m is of French origin as it is accompanied at times by the c/m of a French paper-maker
211	1661	WCL	D 873, c/ms DV & AC in cartouches. Letters so placed indicate French origin
212	1690	CC	
213	1730	CC	
214	1733	CC	W/m of Van der Ley and Honig
215	1776	WCL	D 684, c/m R. Williams
216	1787	CC	
217	1798	CC	
218	1708	WCL	D 688, c/m WK, same c/m as in No. 33

BRITANNIA

219	1750	WCL	D 772, c/m crowned GR
220	1751?		Paper Makers' Association, London, w/m of James Whatman?
221	1760	CC	

222	1762	WCL	D 873
223	1763	WCL	Accounts Vol. LXI, w/m of Joseph Portal?
224	1765	WCL	D 788
225	1764	WCL	Acuocnts Vol. XXXIV, c/m Nind and crowned GR
226	1765	EH	Fenning & Collyer, London, w/m of L. van Gerrevink
227	1769	EH	Legal document, London
228	1773	WCL	D 843
229	1776	EH	Philpotts', Kent, w/m of Tullis Russell & Co., mill No. 10
230	1779	WCL	D 777. Other w/m Garden of Holland. Note the similarity between the two w/ms
231	1787	WCL	D 894
232	1790	CC	
233	1792	EH	Forrest's Mergui Archipelago, London, w/m of J. Whatman?
234	1800	WCL	D 691, w/m of C. Hale
235	1805	WCL	D 767, w/m of Lloyd & Co.
236	ND	WCL	D 600, c/m crowned GR
237	1810	WCL	D 810, w/m of Gilling & Allford
238	1764	WCL	D 863, w/m of C. A. Wessanen and c/m crowned GR

LONDON COAT-OF-ARMS

239	1656		Dugdale's Antiquities of Warwickshire
240	1692	WCL	D 260A, w/m of Abraham Janssen and François Jardel
241	1694	WCL	D 94, w/m of Adriaan Cornelis and Jan Honig
242	1748	CC	W/m of Van der Ley
243	1707	WCL	D 335, w/m of Pieter van der Ley
244	1765	WCL	D 221, w/m of J. Villedary

ROYAL CIPHERS, AND BELL

245	1702		PRO	SP 34/1 f 100, c/m of Elliston & Basket c/m stands for Wilhelmus Rex
246	1706		PRO	SP 34/8 f 56, w/m Arms of England,
247	1704		PRO	SP 34/5 f 12, c/m stands for Anna Regina
248	1764		WCL	Accounts Vol. 1764, w/m Britannia
249	1773		WCL	Accounts Vol. 1773, w/m Britannia
250	ND			End paper
251	1696		CC	
252	1775		WCL	
253	1765		WCL	W/m of L. van Gerrevink 253 "JOB"is an unintentional debasement for "JURÉ"
254	1720		EH	Pety's Atlas of Ireland. Lettering GMT is of Genoese origin
255	ND		CC	
256	1732	MS.	CC	C/m crowned GR
257	1746		PRO	SP 71/18

FRANCE, HOLLAND, ENGLAND, ETC.
COATS-OF-ARMS

258	1760			Del Marmol's Dict. des Filigranes. Arms of Portugal, w/m of Adriaan Rogge
259	ND		CC	Arms of Portugal, w/m of Genoese paper maker. Each mark is in the centre of each half sheet
260	1748		SAP	Arms of Portugal, Genoese w/m
261	1740	MS.	CC	Arms of Spain
262	1747	MS.	CC	Arms of Spain. Golden Fleece. Italian w/m
263	1787	MS.	CC	Golden Fleece
264	XVII C	MS.	CC	G. Hole's map of Worcestershire, Arms of Burgundy. Rhenish paper
265	ND		CC	W/m of Nicolas Briott

266	1623	MS.	CC	Arms of Burgundy and Austria. Golden Fleece
267	1644	MS.	CC	Arms of Baden Hochberg, Rhenish paper
268	1620	MS.	CC	Rhenish paper
269	ND		CC	Rhenish paper
270	1612	MS.	CC	Arms of Thann, Alsace
271	1613	MS.	CC	Arms of Baden
272	1607	MS.	CC	Arms of Regensberg
273	1642	MS.	CC	Same
274	1622	MS.	CC	Arms of Wurzburg
275	1620	MS.	CC	Arms of Wurtemburg
276	1621		CC	Same
277	1611		CC	Same
278	1622	MS.	CC	Arms of Berne, w/m of Dürring
279	1630		CC	Same
280	1650		CC	Same
281	1614		CC	Same. Note the three mounts beneath Dürring's three rings
282	XVII C		CC	Arms of Austria
283	1648		CC	Part of the Arms of Basle, w/m of Dürr
284	1627		CC	Leeuwarden City Archives, one of the many w/ms of the Dürr mills of Basle
285	1603		CC	Arms of Basle, w/m of Dürr
286	1630		CC	W/m of Heusler of Basle
287	1633	MS.	CC	Crozier of Basle
288	1655	MS.	CC	W/m of Heusler of Basle
289	1626		CC	Arms of Neuchâtel?
290	1643		CC	Arms of Soleure
291	ND		CC	
292	1675		CC	Arms of Bergen?
293	c 1732			Del Marmol's Dict des Filigranes pp. 76/77; w/m of J. Honig & Zonen
294	1610		CC	
295	1736		CC	

[78]

296	1613	MS.	CC	
297	ND		CC	Lotter's map of Italy, Augsburg
298	ND		CC	
299	c 1650		CC	Design on wrapper at the Amsterdam City Archives. May mean G. G. á Montignac
300	1636		CC	Handvest van de Landen, Leyden
301	1625	MS.	CC	
302	ND		CC	Homan's map of Moravia, pub. Nuremberg
303	ND		CC	Arms of Antwerp?
304	1643		CC	Design on wrapper at Amsterdam City Archives
305	1683			Arms of France and Navarre. Libro del consejo, St. Martin's Monastery, Santiago di Compostella, Spain
306	1652		PRO	Interregnum
307	1660	MS. WCL		D.
308	1690		CC	Arms of France and Navarre
309	1745		SAP	Arms of Genoa
310	1754	MS.	CC	Arms of Savoy. Also MS. of 1795
311	1633		CC	Arms of Lorraine. The upper c/m is the monogram of the Amsterdam importers of German paper
312	1625		CC	

HORN

313	1600		CC	
314	1620		WCL	A. 68, w/m of Giles Duran
315	1623	MS.	WCL	D. Other dates until 1695
316	1680	MS.	CC	w/m of A. Janssen
317	1770	MS.	CC	Notarial Act. At this time Wendelin Riehel's w/m had become commonplace, and was imitated in several countries
318	1724		CC	

[79]

319	1732		CC	Alkemade's Nederlands Displegtigheden, Rotterdam
320	XVIII C			Del Marmol's Dict. des Filigranes, according to which the date of this w/m is given as 1624, but there were no makers of fine paper in England at this time, and the letter B under the crown may well refer to one of the Blauws, 1744—1827
321	1740	Print	CC	
322	ND		CC	The appendage under the shield is Honig's beehive mark
323	1776		WCL	D 842, w/m of L. V. Gerrevink
324	1777		WCL	D 888, w/m of James Whatman
325	ND		CC	
326	ND		CC	After 1717
327	XVIII C		CC	
328	XVIII C		CC	
329	XVIII C		CC	
330	XVIII C		CC	W/m of Blauw & Briel
331	ND		CC	W/m of Sebelle, Ketel & Wassenbergh, and monogram of Adriaan Rogge

POSTILION

332	1776		WCL	D 875, w/m of J. Villedary
333	ND			End paper Cronyk v. Veldenaer, Holland
334	ND		CC	

FOOLSCAP

| 335 | 1610 | | CC | W/m of N. C. Heusler of Basle |
| 336 | 1630 | | | Design on wrapper in Amsterdam City Archives, w/m of Jean Rousselot of Angoumois |

337	1651			MS. in Veere City Archives, w/m of a French paper-maker
338	1621	MS.	CC	
339	1632	MS.	CC	
340	1645			
341	1644	MS.	CC	
342	XVII C		CC	W/m of Dürring of Basle
343	1644		CC	
344	1649	MS.	CC	
345	XVII C		CC	
346	XVII C		CC	
347	XVII C		CC	
348	1672	MS.	WCL	
349	1675		CC	Parliamentary Papers
350	1645		CC	
351	1647		CC	Map engraved by W. Blaeu. This is an exception to foolscap size
352	1681		CC	
353	1675		CC	Parliamentary Papers
354	1660		CC	
355	1656	MS.	CC	
356	1660		CC	
357	1667		CC	
358	1673	MS.	CC	
359	1689		CC	
360	1682		CC	
361	1673		CC	W/m of Pieter v/d Ley. Paper presented to the writer by Messrs. Van Gelder Zonen
362	1675		CC	Same as above
363	1694		CC	W/m of paper made for Gilis v. Hoven
364	1702	MS.	CC	W/m of paper made for A. Janssen by J. Villedary
365	1640		CC	Design on wrapper of paper imported from

[81]

				France by Cornelis & Antonie de Haes of Amsterdam
366	1671		CC	Facsimile of wrapper of paper made at one of the mills of Abr. Janssen. The letters F C are the initials of a French paper-maker who worked for C. de Haes of Amsterdam, c. 1660
367	1692		CC	Fascimile of wrapper for fine Foolscap paper

LILIES

368	1605		CC	
369	1675		SAP	
370	1791		SAP	
371	1666		CC	Print, Bologna
372	1654		CC	Print, Bologna
373	1714		CC	Engraving, Rome
374	1740		SAP	
375	1740		SAP	
376	1735		SAP	
377	1740		SAP	
378	1636		SAP	
379	1637		SAP	
380	1684			Gazophilacium linguae Persarum, Toulouse
381	1617	MS.	CC	
382	1740		SAP	
383	1750		CC	Paper from Genoese mill
384	1789		CC	Same
385	1750		CC	Same
386	1636		EH	Hexham's Mercator, Amsterdam
387	1650			C/m of Leoben Teenyere, maker of paper with Arms of Amsterdam. Amsterdam City Archives

388	1657	MS.	CC	
389	1666	MS.	CC	
390	1679	MS.	CC	This may be the w/m of J. Salmon, Dutch factor of Angoumois
391	1677		CC	Print, Dutch Official Notice
392	1675		CC	Same
393	1674		PRO	SP–1 King William's Chest; c/m of B. Chabon
394	1777	MS.	CC	
395	1684		CC	W/m of Gilis v. Hoven
396	1764		WCL	D 873
397	1758		CC	Map of Utrecht
398	1792		CC	Kasteleyn's translation of De Lalande's work: L'Art de faire le papier, Dordrecht
399	XVIII C		CC	

STRASBURG LILY

400	1624	CC	
401	1625	CC	Print, Dutch Ordinance
402	1677	CC	
403	1686	EH	W/m of Pieter van der Ley. French edition of Dapper's Africa, Amsterdam
404	c 1725	EH	W/m of the "Fortuyn" mill at Zaandyk
405	1733	CC	Atlas of I. Tirion, Amsterdam. Van der Ley w/m
406	1733	CC	Same Atlas, paper from mill at Egmond, Holland
407	1758	CC	Same Atlas
408	1760		Medical work pub. Amsterdam. Honig's w/m is accompanied by c/ms of two celebrated paper-makers: Wendelin Riehel of Basle and J. Villedary of Hattem, Holland

409	ND	CC	The monogram of A. Rogge is in the centre of the paper between the w/m and the c/m
410	1760		Medical work pub. at Amsterdam, w/m most probably of Adriaan Rogge
411	1766	EH	London print, w/m of Lubertus van Gerrevink
412	XVII C	CC	W/m of Claude de George, who worked for Abr. Janssen
413	1775	EH	Jeffreys West Indian Atlas. This may be an English imitation of a Dutch w/m
414	1780	PRO	SP–37/14. It is not known whether paper with this w/m was made by Joseph Portal or by Lubertus van Gerrevink
415	1782		Company's letter to Fort St. George Jan 25, 1782
416	1788	CC	Print. Amnesty Proclamation
417	1789	EH	Jaeger's Grand Atlas, Frankfort
418	ND	CC	
419	ND	CC	
420	XVIII C	CC	Map of Yezo
421	1792	CC	Map of Austrian Netherlands
422	ND	CC	
423	1664	CC	Handvesten der stad Amstelredam
424	1702	PRO	CO–137/45
425	1683	CC	
426	1699	CC	
427	1645	CC	
428	1671	CC	W/m of Etienne Touzeau

STRASBURG BEND & LILY

429	1683	CC	Map of Purmerlandt
430	1686	CC	W/m of Jan Honig

[84]

431	1686		EH	W/m of Jan, Adriaan & Cornelis Honig
432	1686		EH	W/m of Pieter v/d Ley
433	1724		CC	Print
434	XVIII C		CC	Lea's map of Durham, w/m of Gerrevink and Villedary
435	1785		CC	French edition of Capt Cook's Voyages
436	1790		CC	
437	1722		CC	W/m of J. Villedary

EAGLE

438	1633	MS.	CC	Paper from Basle mill
439	XVII C	MS.	CC	Same
440	1652		EH	Local record of Schieland, Holland
441	1681		EH	Ludolf's Ethiopia, Frankfort
442	1657	MS.	CC	Probably w/m of G. Binnigen of Mont-béliard
443	1632	MS.	CC	also MSS. until 1673
444	1673	MS.	CC	W/m of Pierre Bernard who worked for Van Gangelt, Dutch factor in Angoumois
445	XVII C	EH		W/m of T. Dupuy, Profils et Elevations, Aquéduc de Naintenon

PASCAL LAMB

446	1624	MS.	CC	Italian paper
447	1608	MS.	CC	Same
448	1649	MS.	CC	Same
449	1648	MS.	CC	Same
450	1657	MS.	CC	Same
451	1637		CC	Same. Print, Florence
452	1649		SAP	Italian MS. also MSS. until 1731
453	1652	MS.	CC	Italian paper
454	1654	MS.	CC	Same

455	1684		CC	Gazophilacium linguae Persarum, Toulouse. French w/m
456	1657	MS.	CC	German w/m
457	1672		SAP	Italian w/m, which should be reversed

POT (GENERALLY FRENCH)

458	1618		CC	Blank paper
459	1609		CC	Same
460	1611		CC	Same
461			CC	Same
462			CC	Same
463	1650		CC	Same
464	1691		CC	End paper of Flemish work printed on German paper. The w/m accompanied by a c/m looks German. The w/m on the German paper consists of the Arms of Kempten
465	ND		CC	
466	1642		CC	Print, King Charles I, Declaration
467	1628		CC	Same
468	1628		CC	Same
469	1645		CC	Print, King Charles I, Private Letters
470	1648		CC	Same, King Charles I, Declaration
471	1642		CC	Same, King Charles I, Animadvertions
472	1649		CC	Same, King Charles II
473	1736	MS.	CC	

GRAPES (FRENCH)

474	XVII C		CC	Kip's map of Westmorland
475	1710	MS.	SAP	
476	1680	MS.	SAP	
477	1748		CC	
478	1762		CC	De Lalande, L'Art de faire le papier
479	1804	MS.	SAP	

HATS

480	1771	CC	Print, Rome
481	1649		S. Denne's w/m, Archaelogia, Vol. XII, 1796
482	1652	PRO	SP–18/23
483	1652	WCL	D 224
484	1663	WCL	D 873
485	1681	PRO	SP–29/417 f 81. Nos. 481/5 appear to be French w/ms. Denne described the mark as a Puritan's hat

THREE HATS

486	1622	MS.	SAP
487	1624	MS.	CC
488	1700	MS.	CC
489	1671	MS.	SAP
490	1777	MS.	CC
491	1807	MS.	SAP

ROYAL HEADS (FRENCH)

492	1804	CC
493	1810	CC
494	1814	CC

MISCELLANEOUS

495	1662	CC	Frontispiece of Stoppelaar's monograph, w/m of François Chatonet?
496	1662	CC	W/m of Cornelis de Haes, Amsterdam, importer of paper from Angoumois
497	1662	CC	Same
498	1662	CC	Same

499	1631	MS.	CC	C/m "IR", (PRO Interregnum, c/m "MG" 1651)
500	1634	MS.	CC	
501	1626	MS.	CC	
502	1672		SAP	Italian paper, with c/m in right hand corner
503	1675		SAP	Same
504	XVII C			Bagford's Collection, British Museum
505	1638			Wrapper in Amsterdam City Archives with the following inscription: "Papier fin fait par Jean Roulet á son moulin du Got" PRO SP–18/94 f 48, c/m IR
506	1650	MS.	SAP	Italian paper
507	1662	MS.	CC	Same
508	1800	MS.	CC	Spanish paper?
509	1686	MS.	CC	W/m of Wendelsteiner mill, Bavaria
510	ND	MS.	CC	German paper
511	ND	MS.	CC	Same
512	1644		CC	Atlas of the Netherlands, J. Blaeu
513	XVII C			Bagford's Collection, British Museum
514	XVIII C		CC	Reprint of a map of France dated 1713 on paper watermarked 1742, according to w/m of J. Dupuy
515				C/m of No. 514
516	1743		CC	Map of N. France, Paris, same w/m as tracing No. 514
517				Wrapper from Bagford's Collection, British Museum. Harleian Lib. No. 5942. (Trans: Extra Superfine paper)
518	1628			Bible printed in London. French w/m
519	ND		CC	W/m of Heusler of Basle
520	1695		CC	Mordan's map of Durham. Camden's Britannia

521	1637		WCL	D. Lloyd's Memoirs
522	1656	MS.	CC	Italian paper
523	1700	MS.	CC	Same
524	1700	MS.	SAP	Italian paper
525	1640		CC	Print, Charles I, Declaration
526	1691		CC	Same, same Declaration
527	1640		CC	Same, same Declaration
528	1653			End paper of incunabulum, King's Coll. Cambridge
529	1640		CC	Print, Charles I, Declaration
530	1625		PRO	SP–16/521, eye copy
531	1664		WCL	D–MS
532	1722		CC	W/m on maps in Camden's Britannia, Genoese w/ms
533	1722		CC	W/ms on maps in Camden's Britannia, in one of the two editions of 1722. Letters G.M.T. appear on paper made in Genoa
534	1740		SAP	Letter T resembles the same letter in No. 533. This w/m is Italian
535	1695		CC	C/ms in Camden's Britannia. The spectacles and lettering are peculiarly Genoese

INITIALS

536	1794		CC	J. Walch's map of Holland
537	ND		CC	Stout, light brown paper
538	ND		CC	W/m of J. Villedary
539	XVII C		CC	Tellière w/m
540	XVIII C		CC	These Tellière w/ms are mentioned in the French Law of 1741, regulating the sizes and weights of paper

[89]

UNDETERMINED (FRENCH)

541	1736		CC	Book concerning medals, Amsterdam
542	1770		CC	Print
543	1773		CC	Print
544	1640		CC	
545	1620	MS.	CC	

OFFICIAL STAMPED PAPER

546	1776–1815	CC	French

FRENCH IMITATIONS OF GENOESE WATERMARKS

547/50	XVIII C	W/ms from MSS. at the Library of St. Martin's Monastery at Santiago di Compostella, Spain

COUNTERMARKS AT EACH CORNER OF PAPER

551	XVIII C	W/m of Giacomo Gambino of Genoa
552	XVIII C	W/m of Giambatista Fabiani of Genoa

DOUBLE CHAIN WATERMARKS

553	1599	MS.	CC	Genoese w/m (3 mondi)
554	1655	MS.	CC	Genoese w/m, same
555	1676	MS.	CC	Genoese w/m
556	1695	MS.	CC	Genoese w/m
557	1744	MS.	SAP	Genoese w/m

DATED PAPER

547/50	XVIIIC	French imitations of Genoese w/m
558	1653	End paper of an incunabulum
559	1737	Genoese w/m

560	1739				Genoese w/m
561	1741				Specimen from book published in Geneva
562	1742				"Antiquités d'Arles", dated 1687
563/4	1772-1773	MS.	CC		Italian paper
565	1796				W/m of William Lepard, in Archaeologia. Vol. XII, 1796

WATERMARKS IN ALLUSION TO SURNAMES OF PAPER-MAKERS

566	1700		CC	(Honey)	W/m of Honig
567	XVIII C			(Well)	W/m of Dupuy, from No. 29 in Sources of Information (p. 90)
568	1665		CC	(Hare)	W/m of Haes
569	1791	MS.	CC	(Little leg)	W/m of Gambino
570	1787	MS,	CC	(Head)	W/m of Testa
571	1786	MS.	CC	(Leg)	W/m of Gambino
572	1782	MS.	CC	(Fish)	W/m of Rogge
573	1794	MS.	CC	(Hare)	W/m of Leveratto
574	1619	MS.	CC	(Letter B)	W/m of Le Be
575	1625	MS.	CC	(House)	W/m of Heusler
576	1803	MS.	CC	(Leek)	W/m of Porrata
577	1810		SAP	(Vineyards)	W/m of Vignals
578	1800	MS.	CC	(Just)	W/m of Giusti

SOME OF THE AUTHORITIES CONSULTED AND SOURCES OF INFORMATION

1   L'Histoire du Papier, by Augustin Blanchet, Paris, 1900
2   Handvesten, Privilegien, enz., der Stad Amstelredam, 1663
3   "Hollandsche Papier", by J. W. Enschedé, 1922
4   Proefnemingen om Papier te maken zonder Lompen, (Paper making without rags). Dutch translation from the German of J. C. Schäffer of Ratisbon, Amsterdam, 1770
5   "Invention of Paper" &c. by Matthias Koops, London, 1801, p. 241
6   "Het Papier", by J. H. de Stoppelaar, Middelburg, 1869
7   "Les Filigranes", by C. M. Briquet, Leipzig, 1923
8   Paper wrappers at the Amsterdam City Archives
9   "Recherches sur l'origine des moulins à Papier de l'Angoumois", by G. Babinet de Rencogne, Angoulême, 1880
10 Dutch Ordinances of the Province of Groningen, 1618—1797
11 "De Papiermaker", by P. J. Kasteleyn, translation from the French of De Lalande, published by A. Blussé en Zoon, Dordrecht, 1792
12 Maps and Atlases engraved by Willem Blaeu, Isaac Tirion, I. Covens and C. Mortier
13 "Dans l'herbe des trois vallées", by Henri Pourrat, Paris, 1927
14 "L'Art de faire le Papier", by De Lalande, Paris, 1762
15 "Le Papier", by Louis Le Clert, Paris, 1926, p. 51
16 Papier en papierhandel in N. Nederland ged. de 17e eeuw, Published in Tydschrift voor boek en bibliotheekwezen 1909, by J. W. Enschedé
17 "Geschichte der Papiermühlen", by Dr. Albert Jaffé, Pirmasens, 1933
18 "Het Huis", Oud en nieuw, by J. G. Honig, Amsterdam, 1927
19 L'Industrie du Papier à Angoulême, by Maurice Tiffon
20 "De Geschiedenis der Nederlandsche Papierindustrie", by E. G. Volkersz
21 Cambridge History of English Literature, Vol. II, p. 323
22 Public Record Office. Examination of 20,000 MSS

23 "Paper and Paper Making", by R. Herring, London 1853
24 "Papermaking through Eighteen Centuries by Dard Hunter, New York, 1930
25 Public Record Office, State Papers 32/3 f 209 et seq.
26 Haydn's Dictionary of Dates, 23rd Ed. 1903
27 "Les premières papeteries françaises", by Henri Alibaux, Paris, 1926
28 "Les origines du papier", by André Blum, Paris, 1932
29 "Papeterie et Papetiers de l'ancien temps", by J. Grand-Carteret, Paris, 1913
30 "Les papeteries des environs de Morlaix", by H. Bourde de la Rogerie. Bulletin Historique, Paris, 1911
31 "Papyrus sive Ars conficiendae Papyri", by J. Imberdis Claramonte, MDCXCIII

AMSTERDAM

1

I M

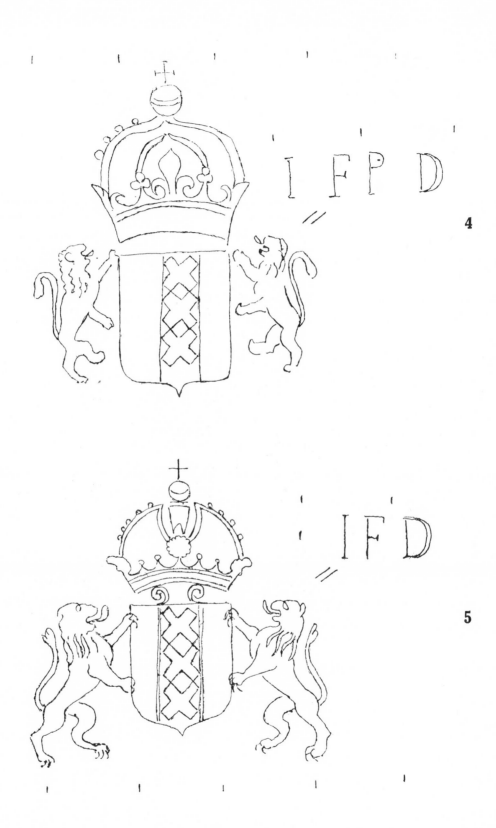

4

5

P. D.

6

7

PB

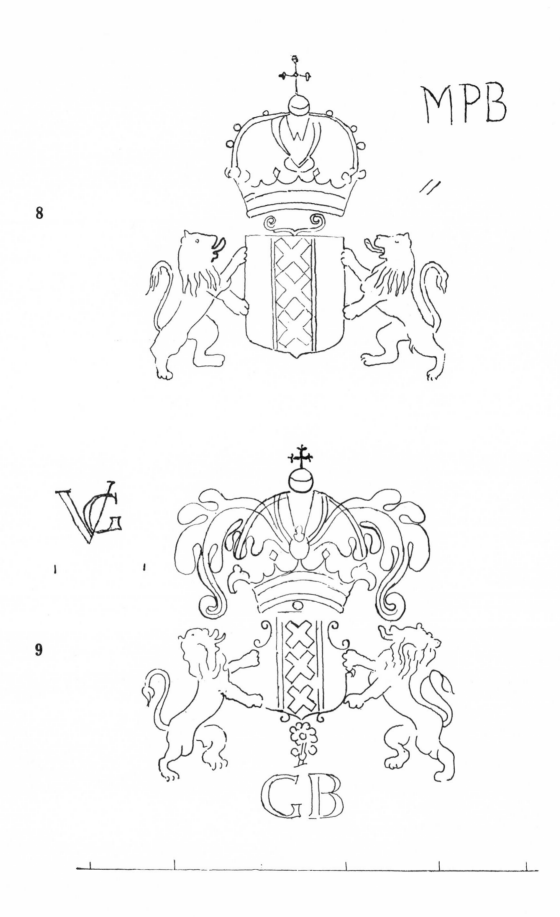

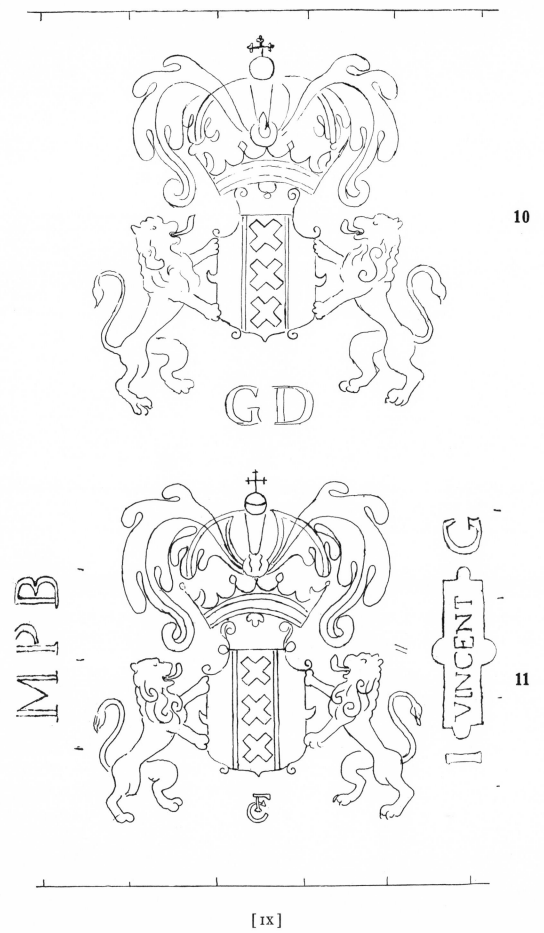

10

11

Watermarks in paper.

2

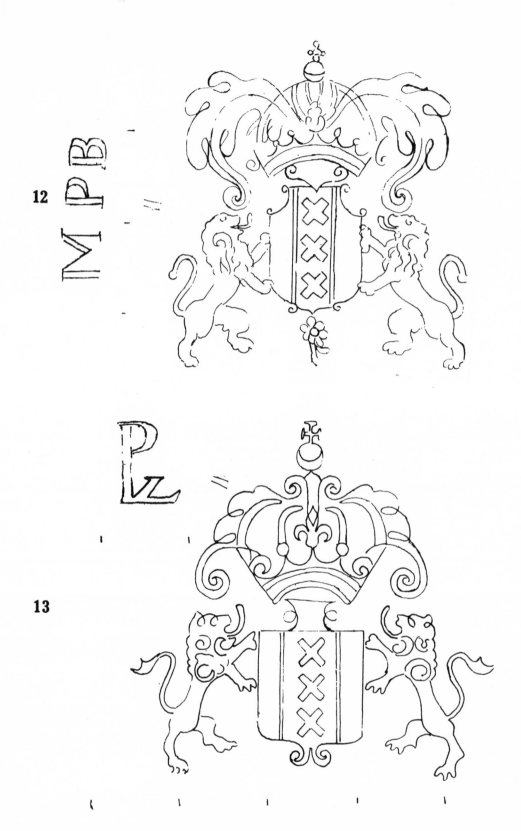

12

13

14

P D

15

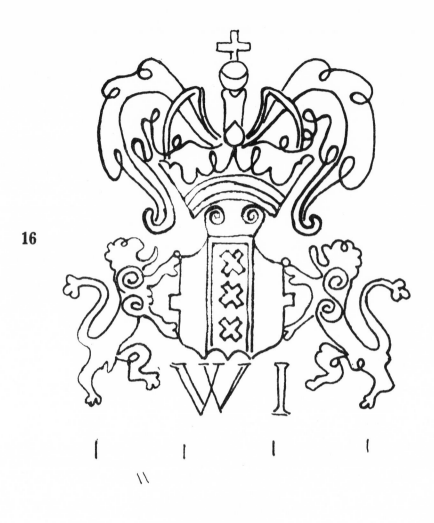

16

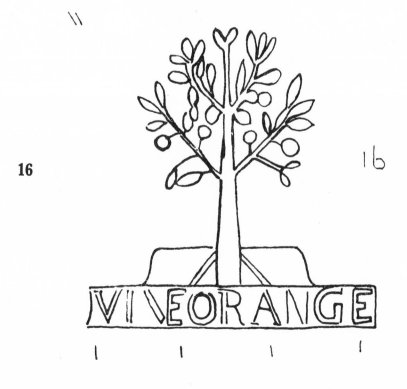

16   16

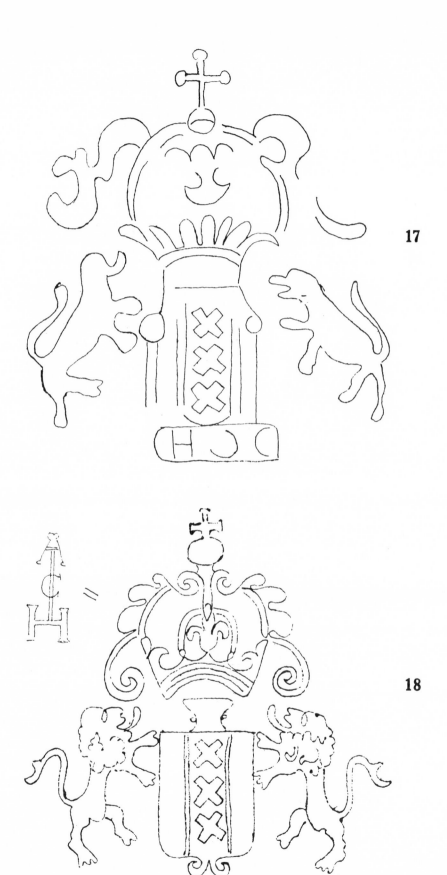

17

18

19

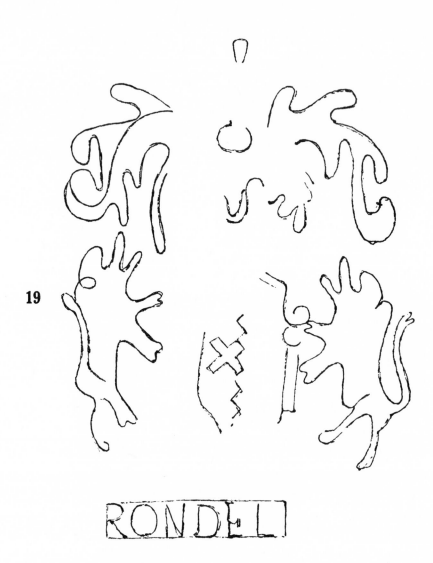

RONDELI

20

21

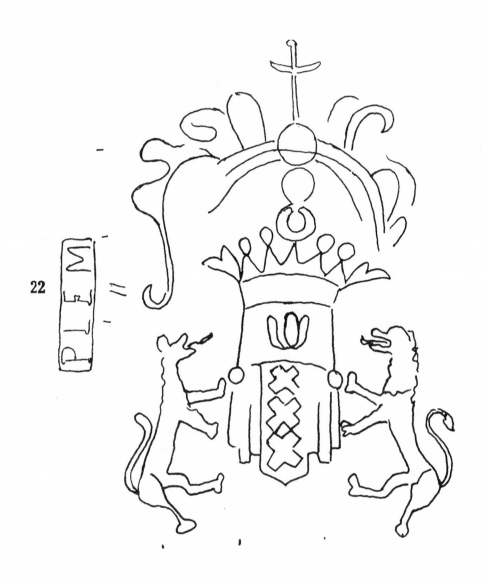

22

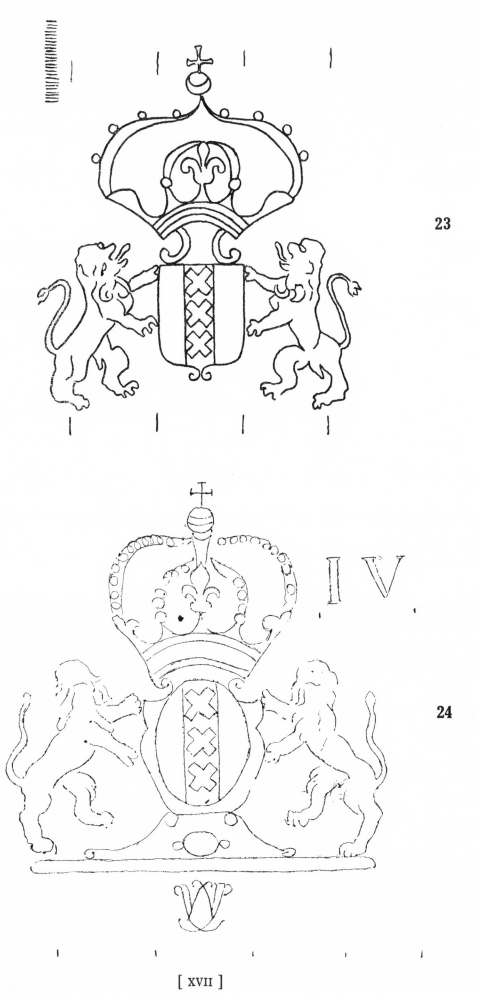

23

IV.

24

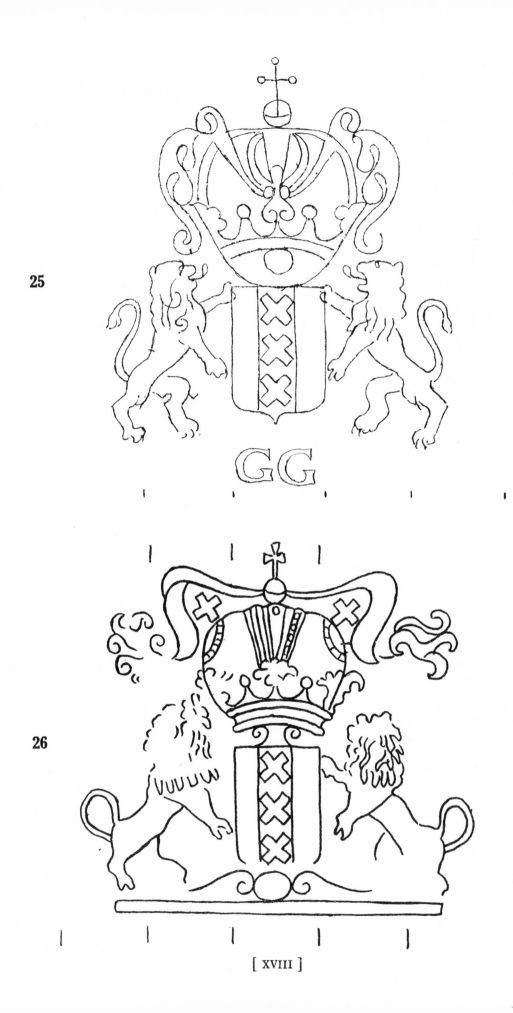

25

26

27

28

29

30

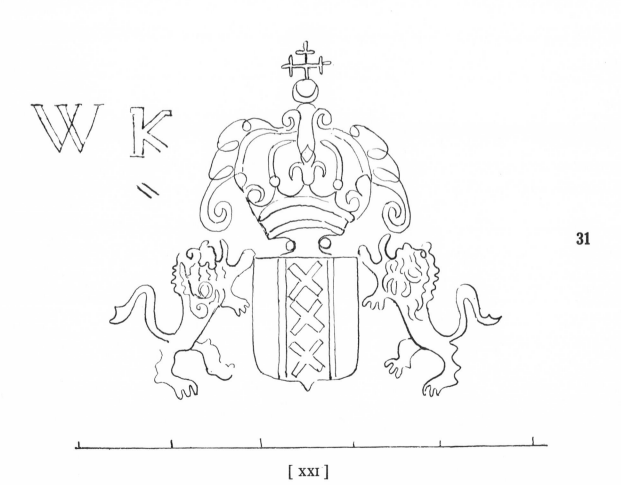

31

32

33

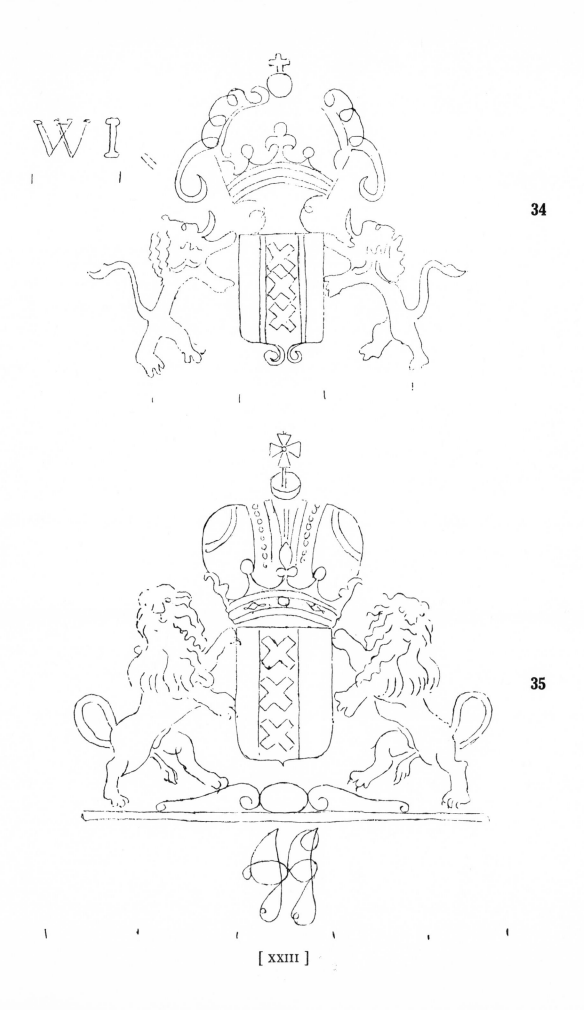

34

35

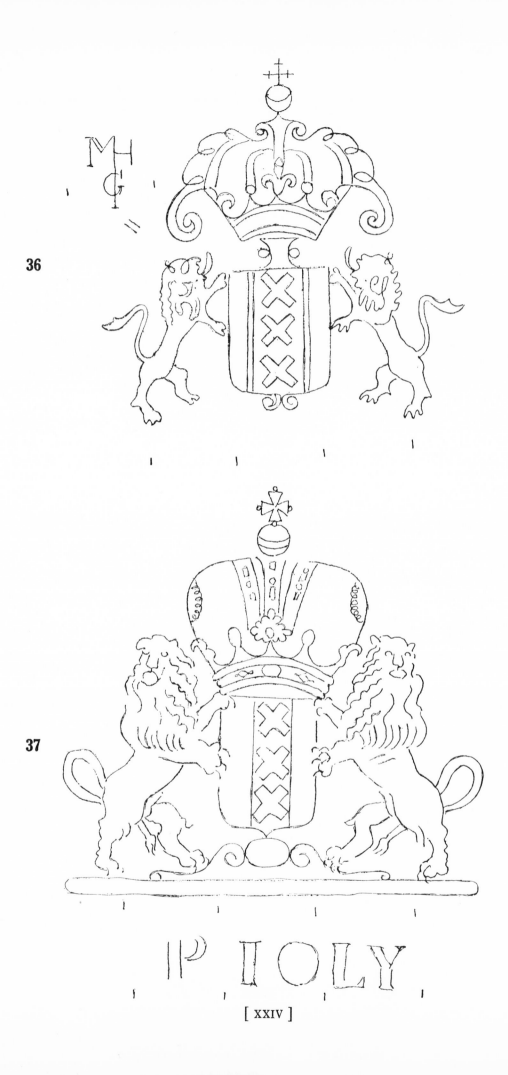

36

37

ℙ ℐOLY

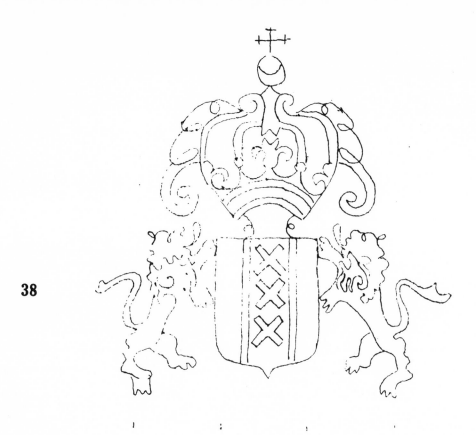

38

IAN VAN TIL

39

[XXV]

40

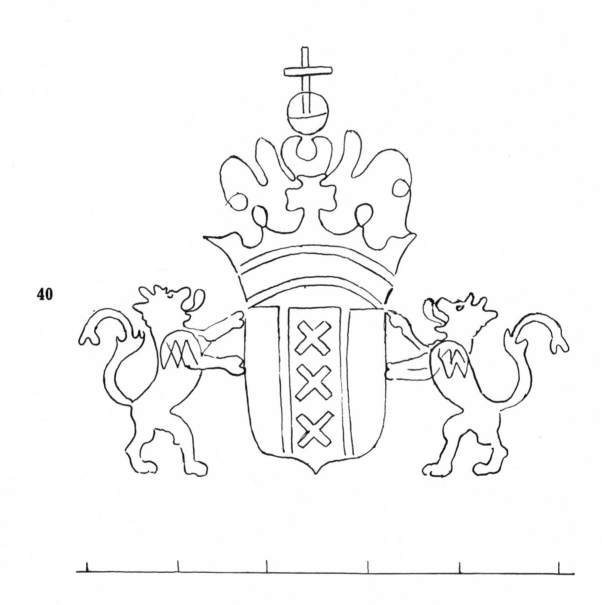

41

IUILLEDARY

42

BEAÜVAIS

43

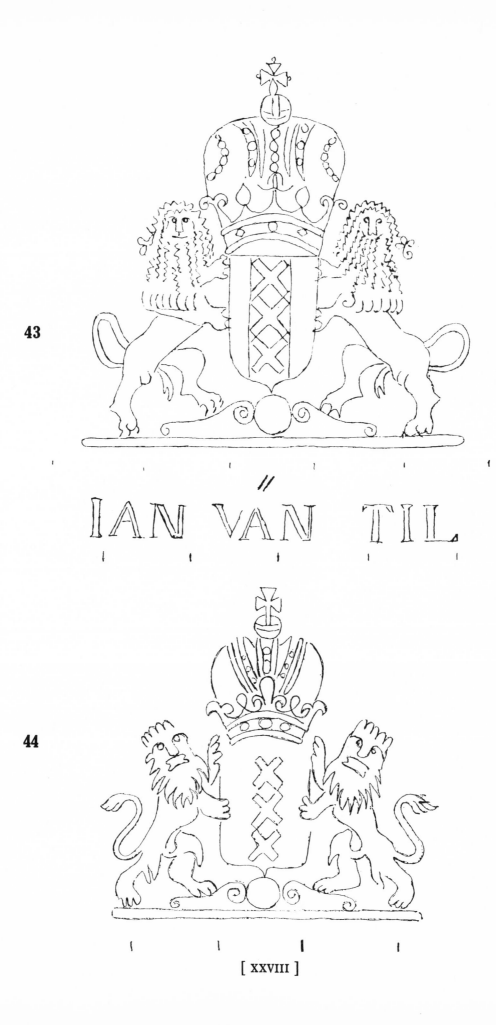

44

45

P TARVIAVD

46

47

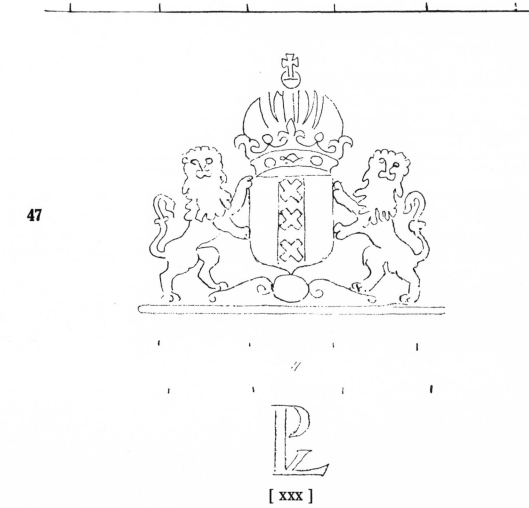

48

49

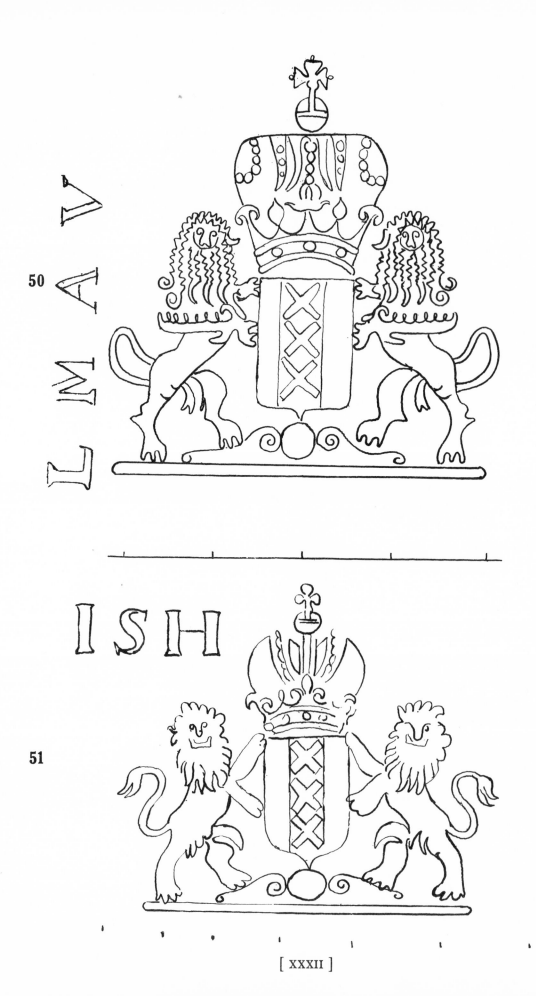

50

51

52

LVG

I VILLEDARY

[XXXIII]

53

MARCHAIX

54

55

II D(o)RT

DIT IS OPRECHT VELUS

[xxxv]

56

1742

R HARDEL
FIN
PERIGORD

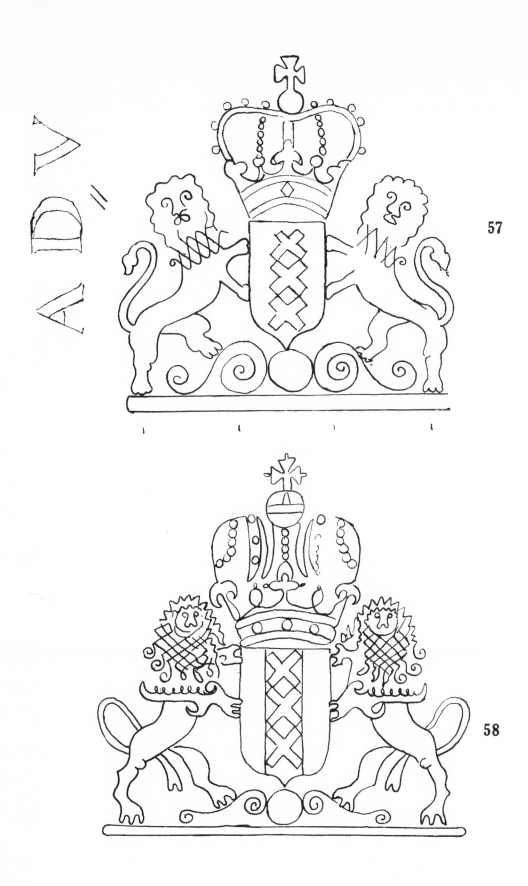

57

58

Amsterdam Clota

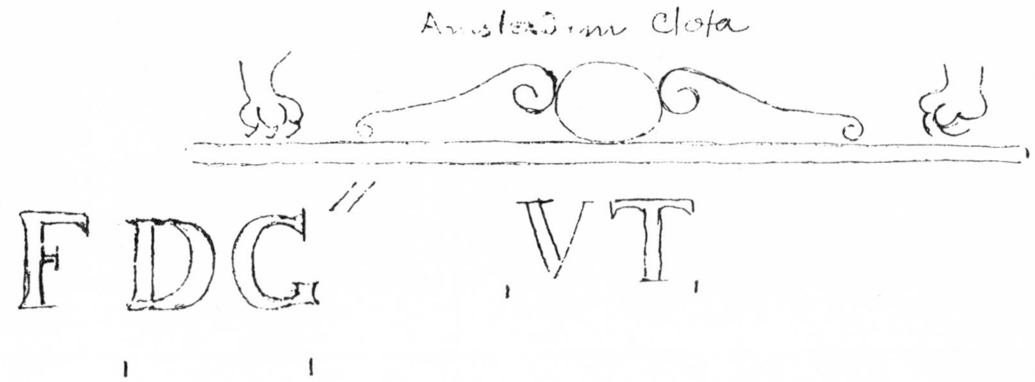

59   F D G"   V T

60   I S

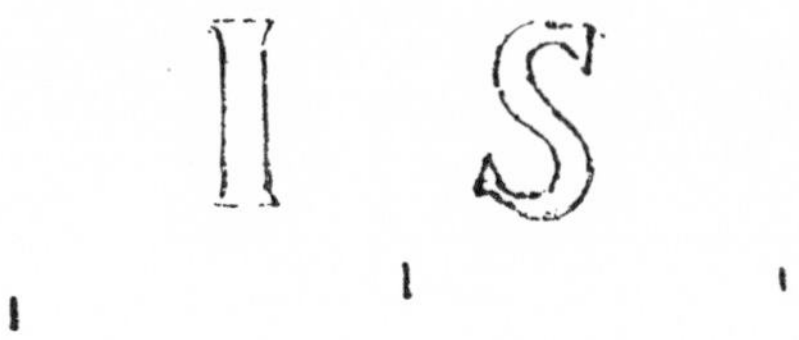

61   V D   =   ✕

62   D I .   =   A I

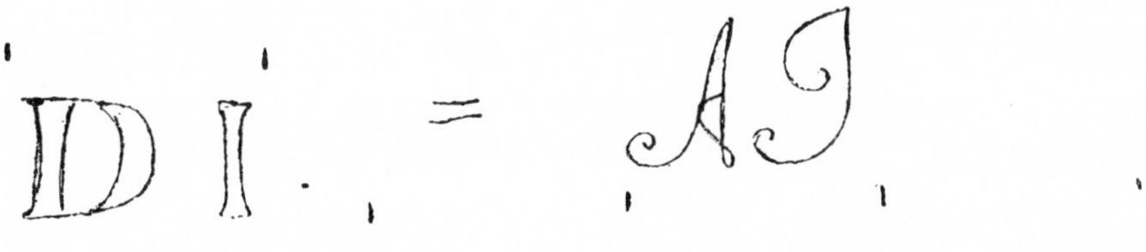

63   N M C

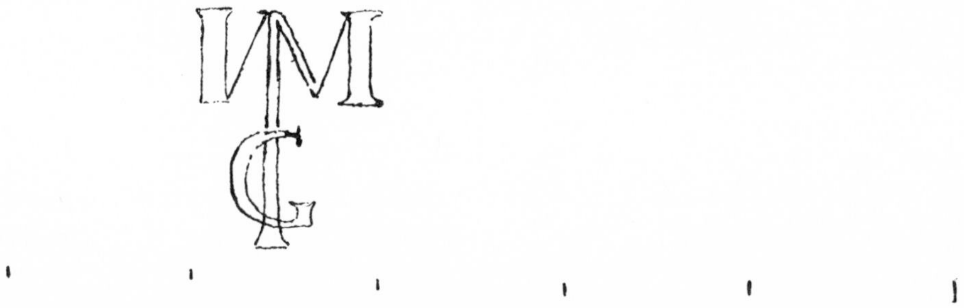

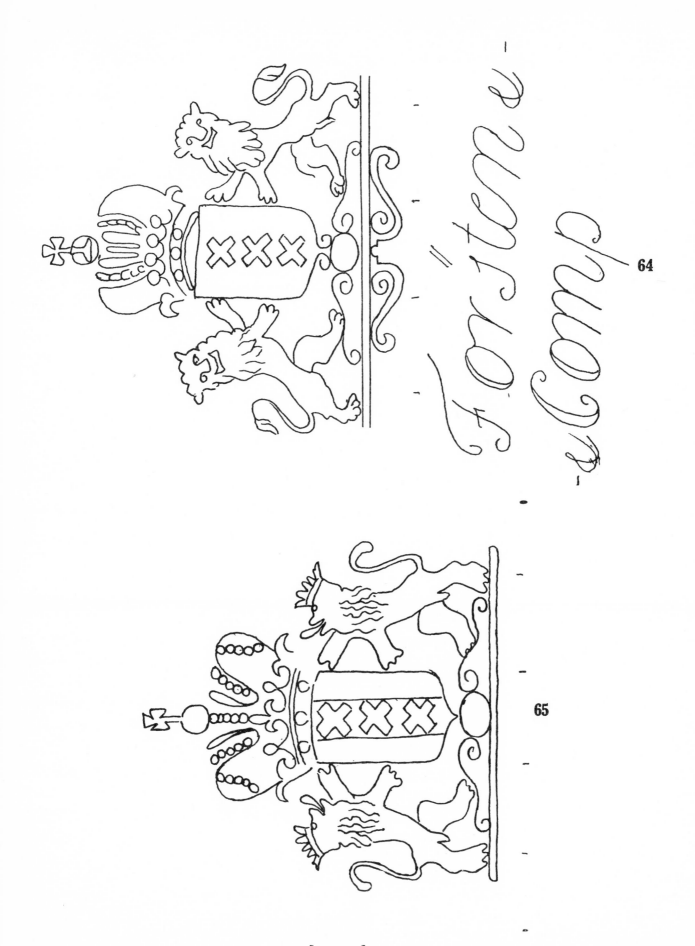

64

Forsten &
Comp

65

66

P B

P Brouwer

[XL]

H·BROUWER
& COMP

67

68

[XLI]

69

BOVYGVE

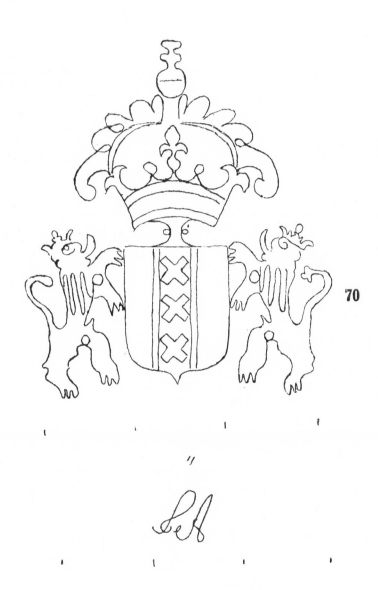

70

71

R IAR DEL
1742

72

D JARDEL

[XLIV]

AM VG

73

74

P RIVIÈRE

[XLV]

75

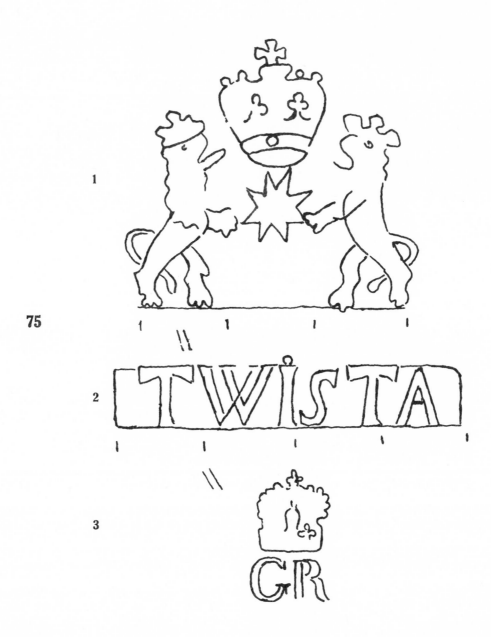

1

2

3

76

77

78

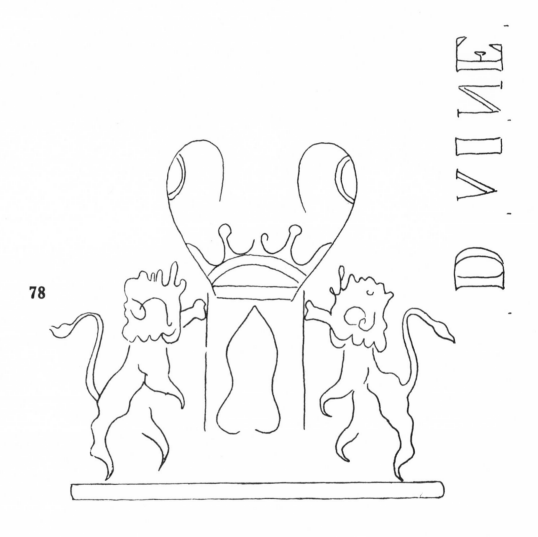

D. VIVE.

VRYHEYT

79

80

ADRIAAN ROGGE

81

PRO PATRIA EIUSQUE LIBERTATE

VRYHEYT

82

D & C BLAUW

PRO PATRIA EIUSQ UE LIBERTATE

VRYHEYT

B

83

AS

84

85

85a

86

VAN DER LEY

Watermarks in paper.

87

PRO PATRIA EIUSQUE LIBERTATE

VRYHEID

C & I HONIG

[LVIII]

88

89

[LX]

90

W & Pannekoek

91

92

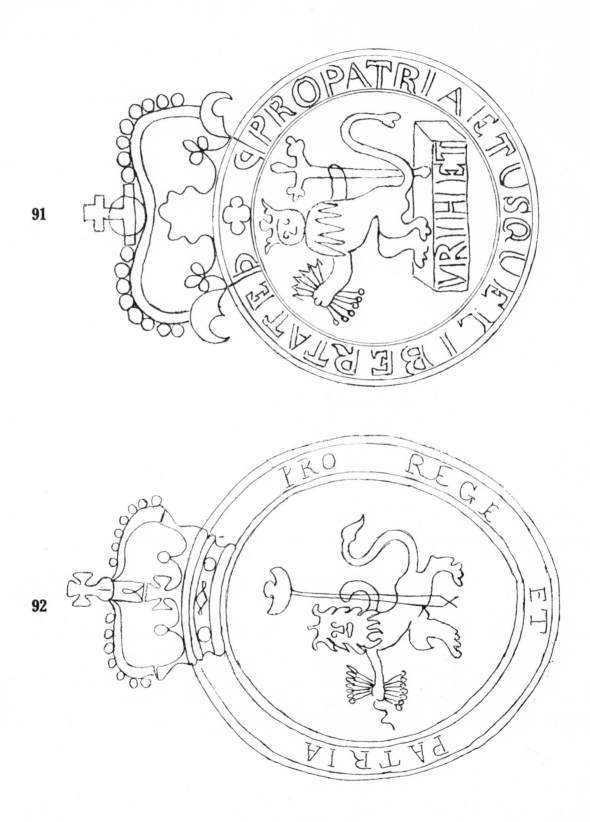

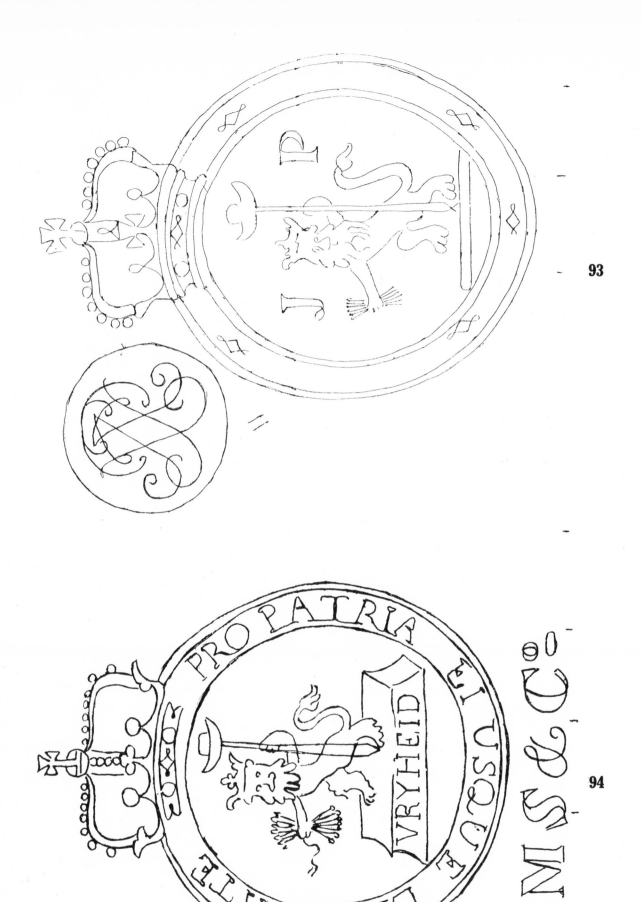

93

94

95

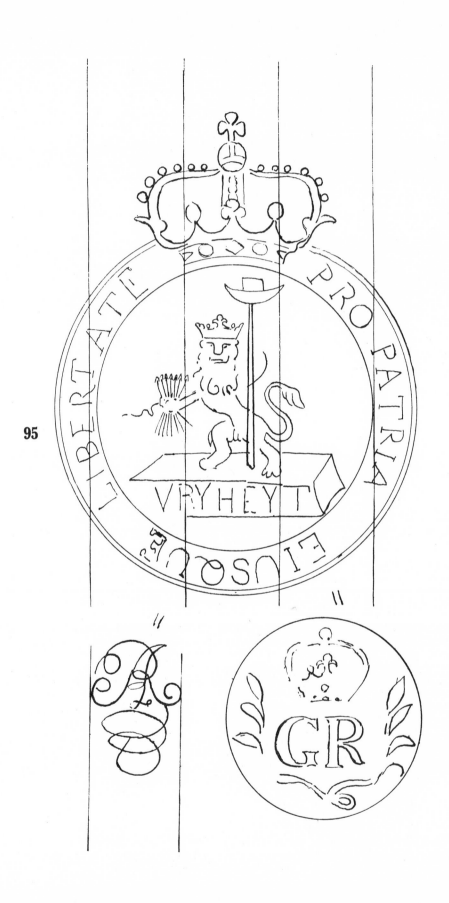

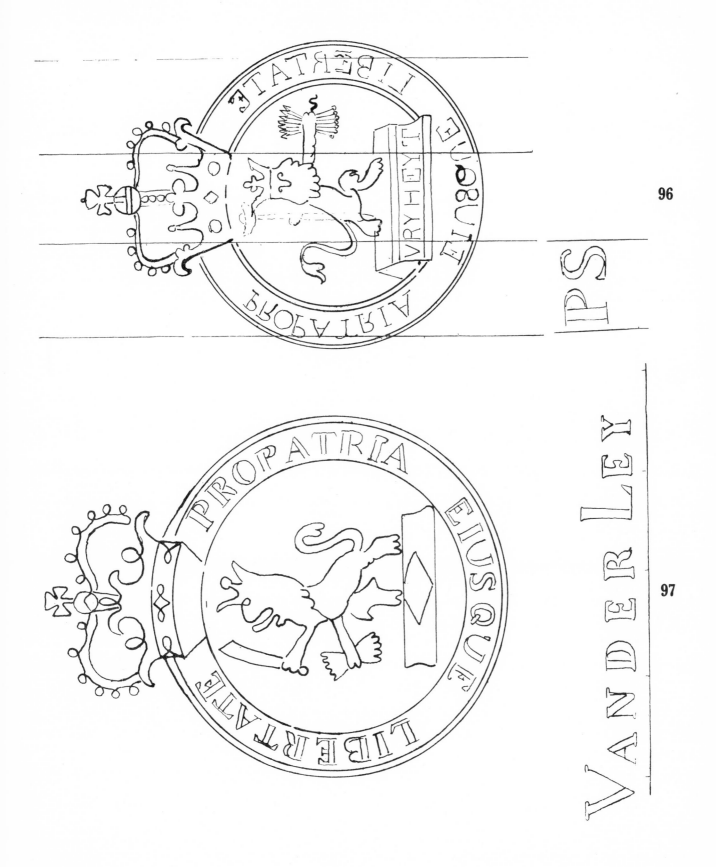

96

97

PS

VAN DER LEY

[LXV]

Watermarks in paper.

98

W. W & HPANNEKOEK

99

J. Kloppenburg

100

GIB

VAN KEMPEN & C.

101

102

K & D

103

PANNEKOEK

104

105

3

FEUILLETAU DE BRUYN
& C^E

[LXXIII]

Watermarks in paper.

106

T Sanders & Zoon

107

108

SEVEN PROVINCES

111

112

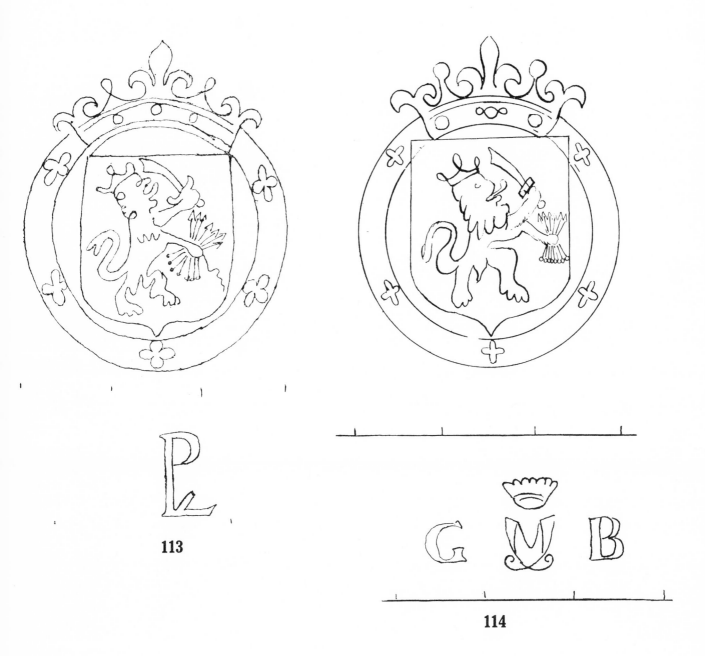

113

114

Watermarks in paper.

115

116

117

I V

118

119

JH & Z
120

K & D
121

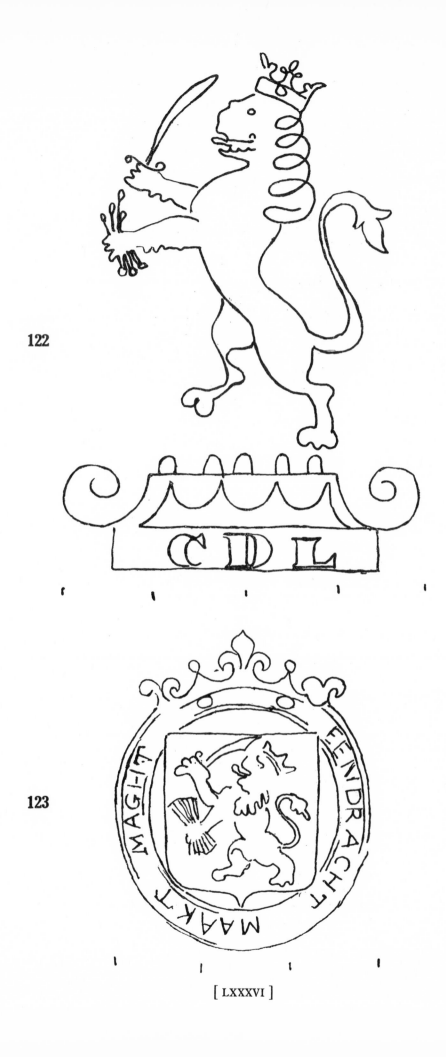

122

123

124

V D L

125

VAN GELDER

126

Watermarks in paper.

PRO PATRIA

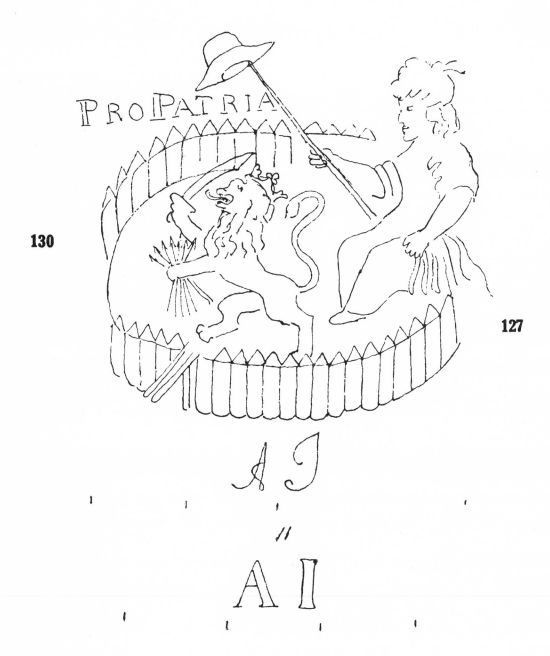

130

127

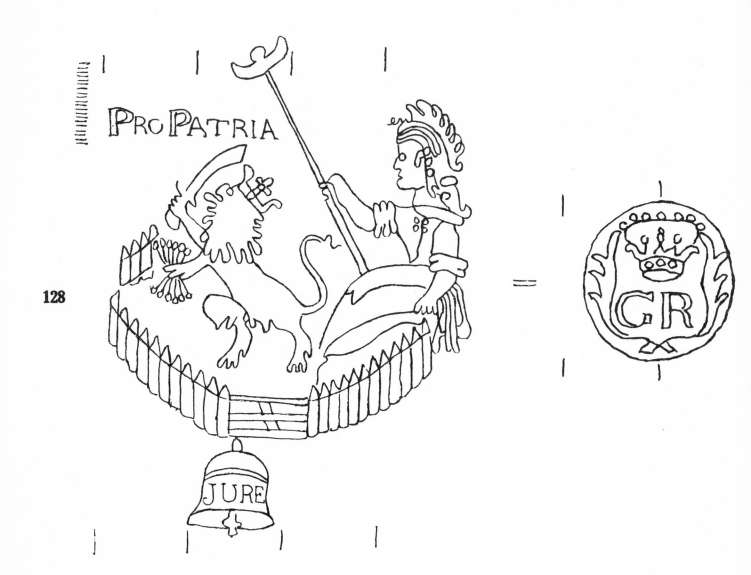

128

PRO PATRIA

JURE

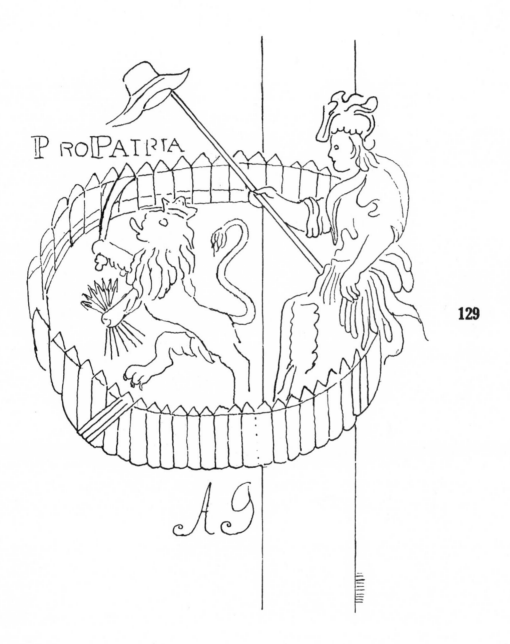

PROPATRIA

129

A9

PRO PATRIA

IⅤL

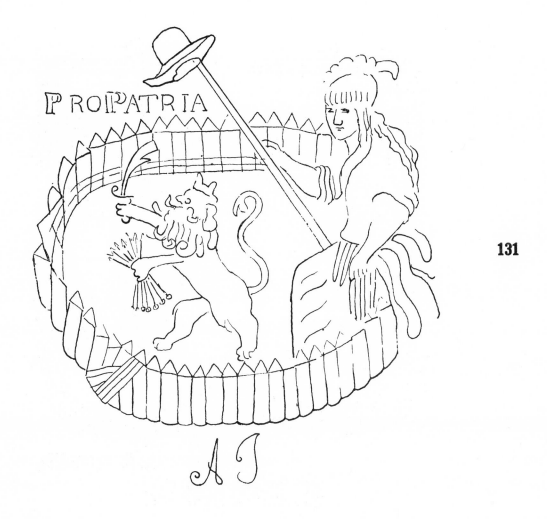

131

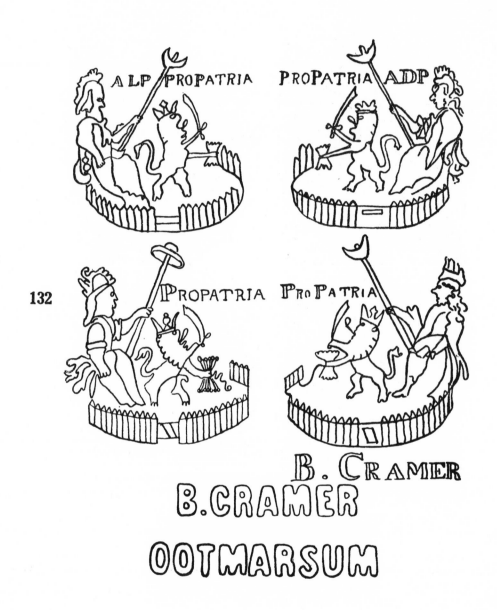

132

PRO PATRIA

133

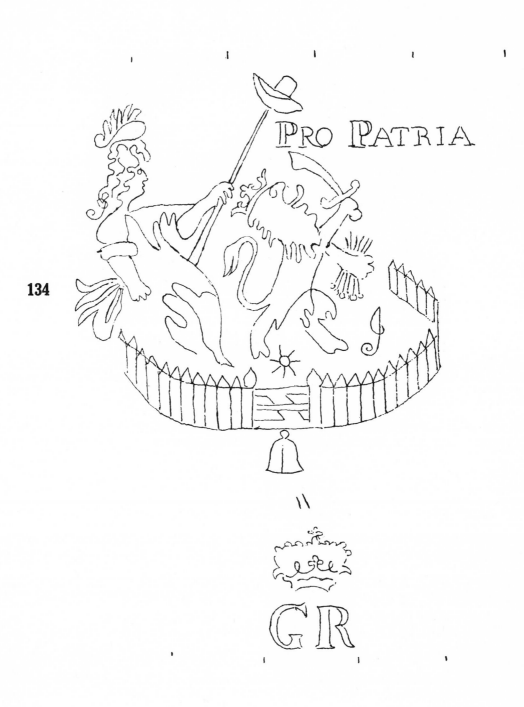

134

PRO PATRIA

GR

[C]

PRO PATRIA

135

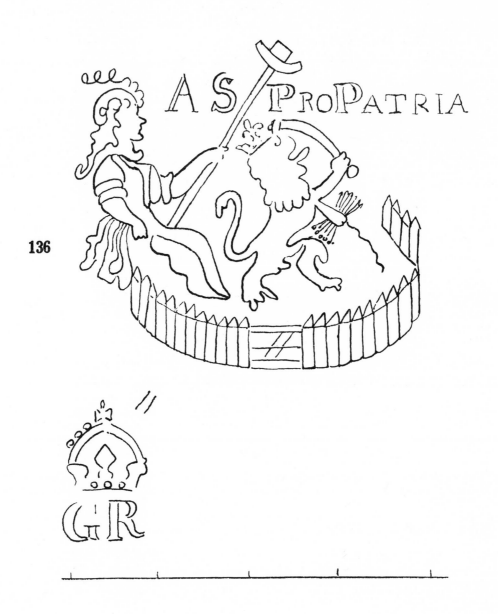

136

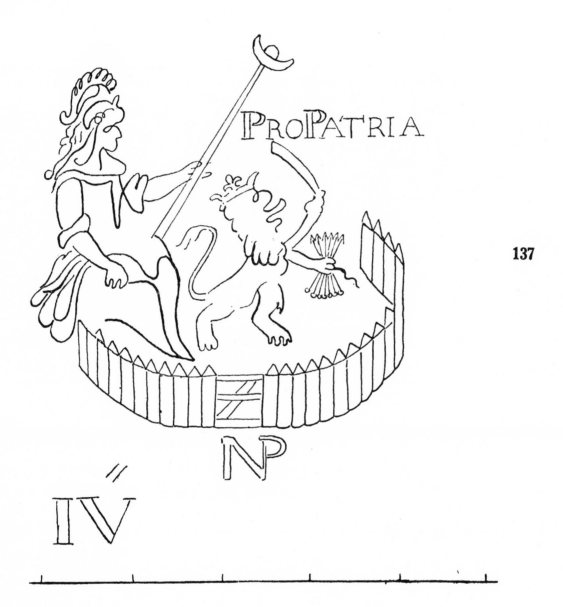

137

POUR L'ANGLETERRE

138

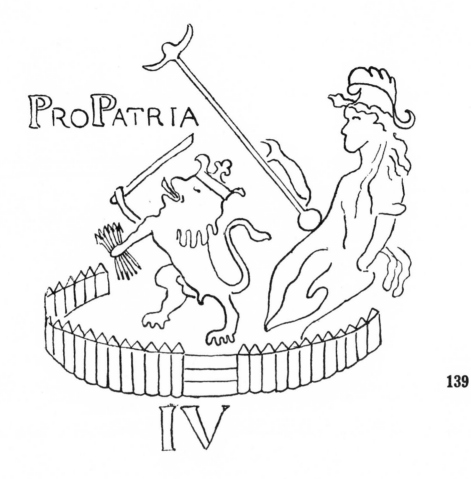

PROPATRIA

IV

139

GR

[CV]

DURHAM

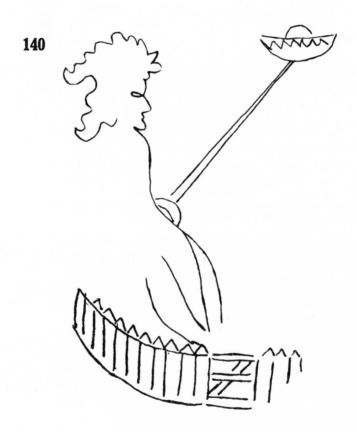

140

PROPATRIA

141

HC HOYSING

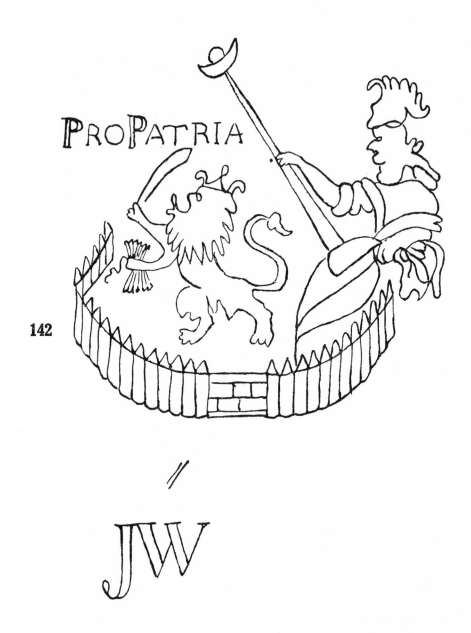

142

PRO PATRIA

JW

ProPatria

143

ProPatria

144

T·French

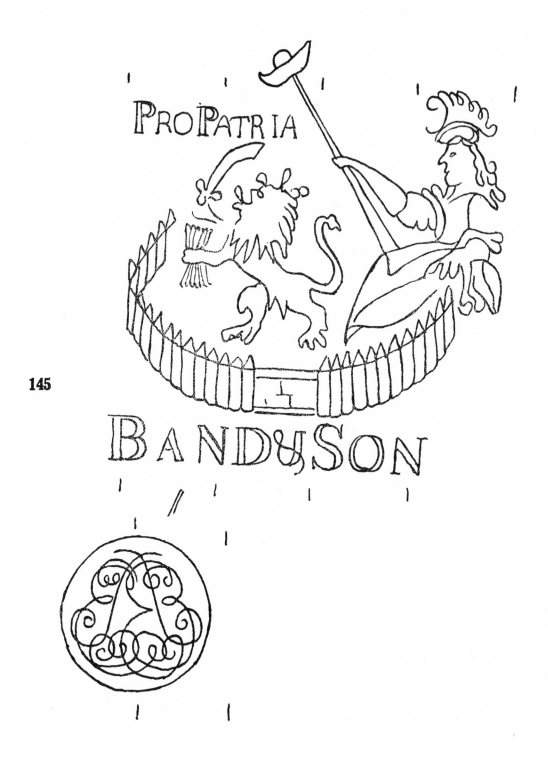

145

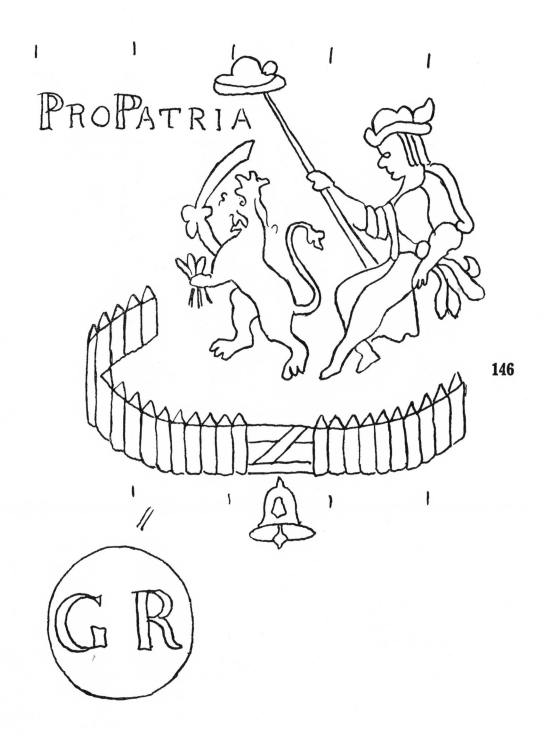

146

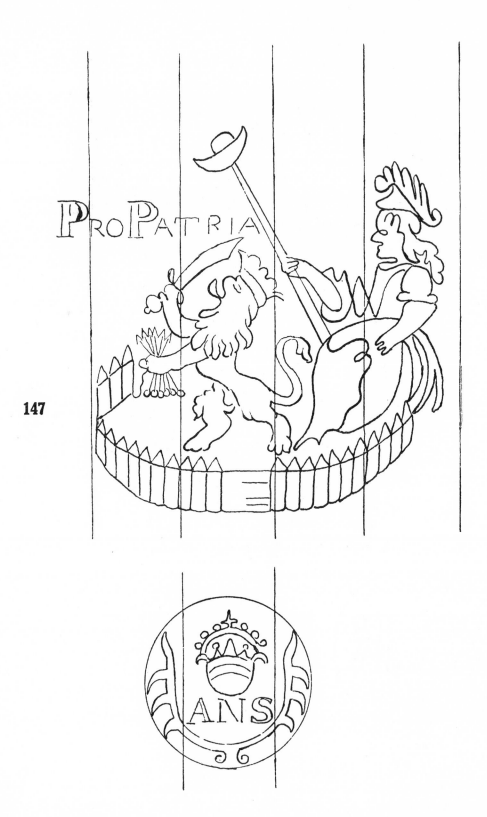

147

PRO PATRIA

ANS

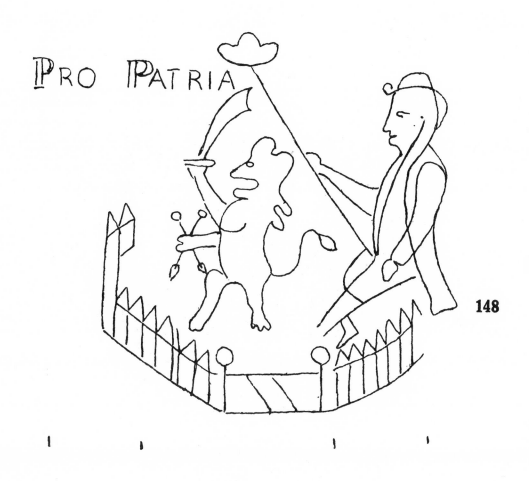

148

Watermarks in paper.

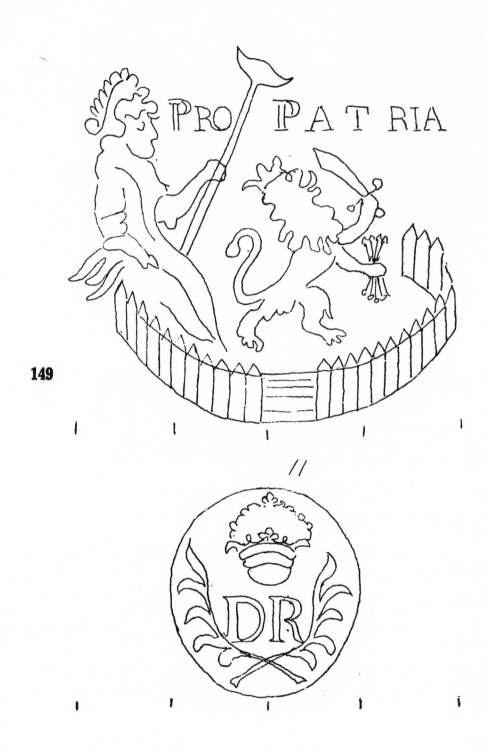

149

PRO PATRIA

C: I: MEYRINK.

150

CIM

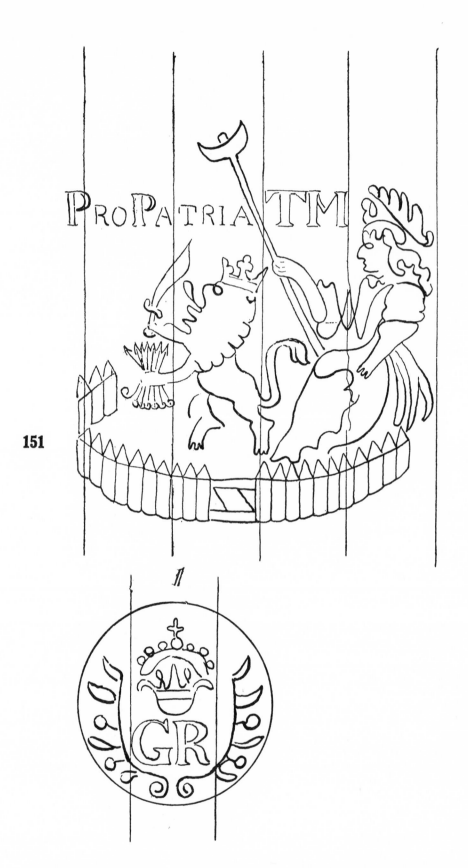

151

1

SOCIETATE BOXTEL

PROPATRIA

H Kamphuis KID **152**

Molekaten

GR

[CXVII]

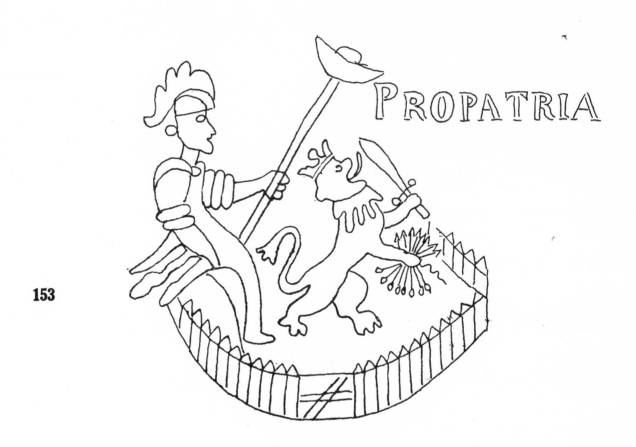

153

PROPATRIA

ARMS OF ORANGE NASSAU

154

155

WILLEM
DEVYFDE
IV

[CXXII]

156

WILLEM · DE · VYFDE

157

W ILLEM
D E V YFDE

H C H OISING

LIONS (CONCORDIA, ETC.)

158

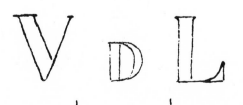

159

CRESCUNT CONCORDIA RESPARVAE

M van LIER & ZOON

161

Watermarks in paper.

162

ANGLO DUTCH COATS-OF-ARMS

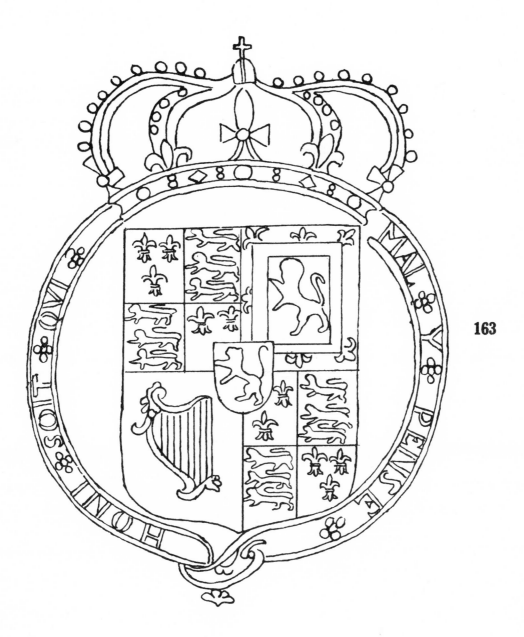

163

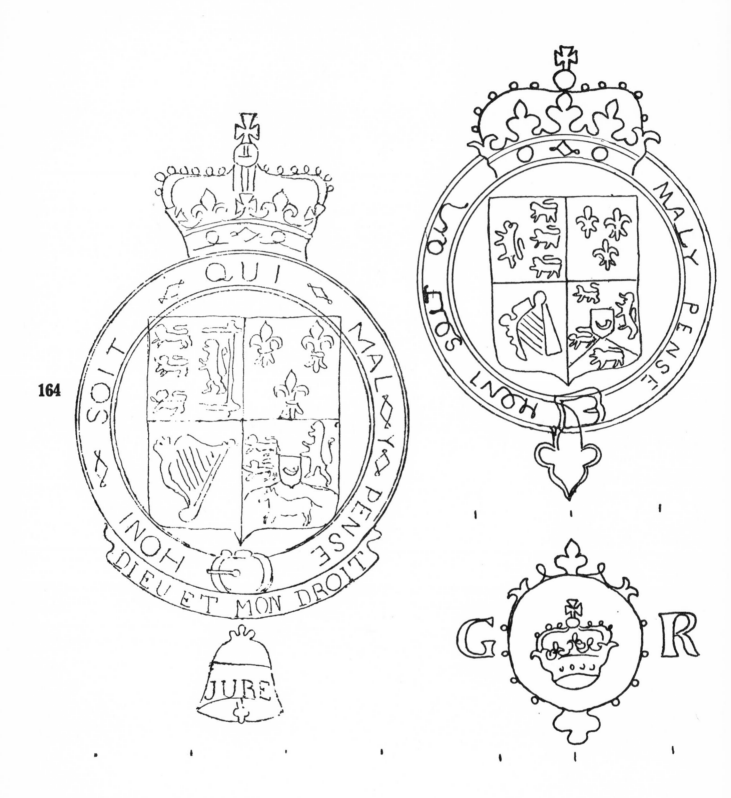

164

DUTCH ROYALTIES

166

Watermarks in paper.

167

P W de Veyfde

Kouwenhoven

168

PW DE VYFDE

D & C BLAUW

169

170

WILLEM FREDERIK
ERF P.V.ORANJEN

FORSTEN EN COMP.

171

PRINS WILLEM
DE WFDE

172

VANDERLEY

173

JH & Z

[CXLIV]

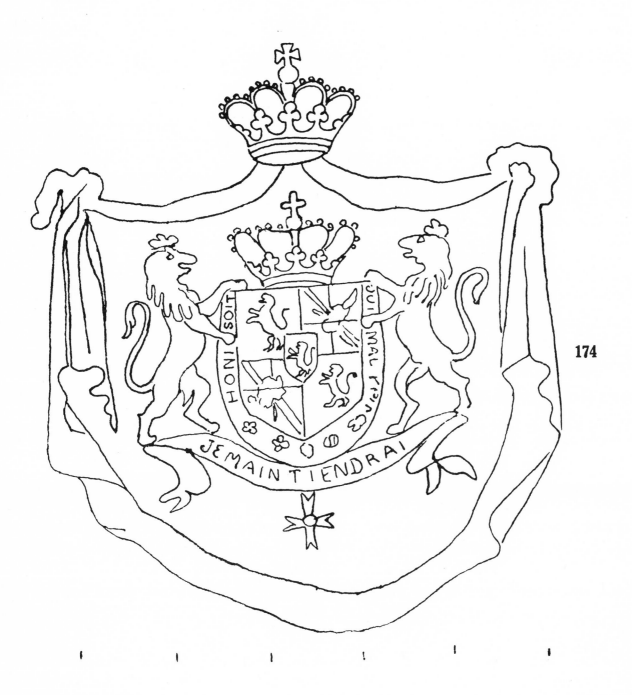

174

Watermarks in paper.

175

HONIG

DUTCH PROVINCES AND CITIES

176

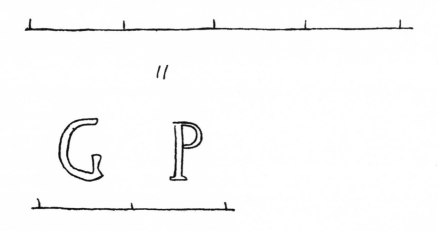

177

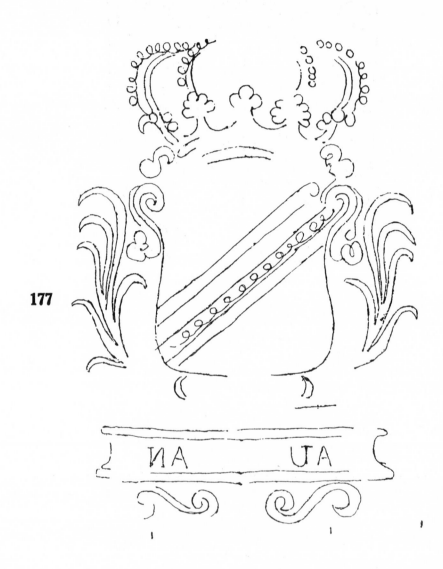

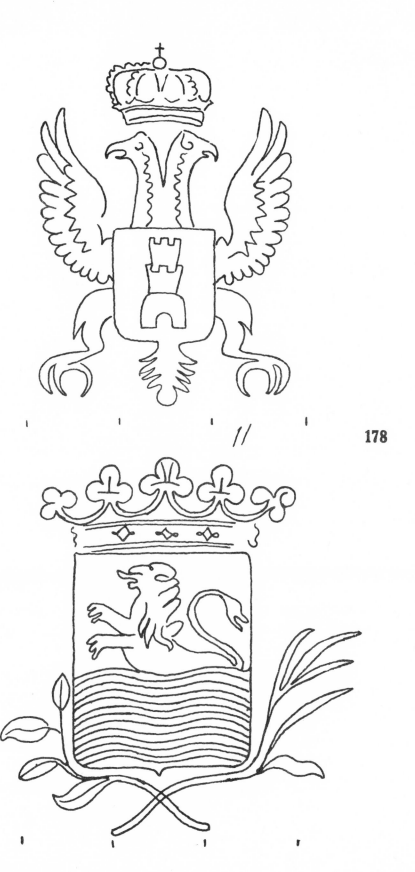

178

BEEHIVE

179

180

HONI

J H & Z

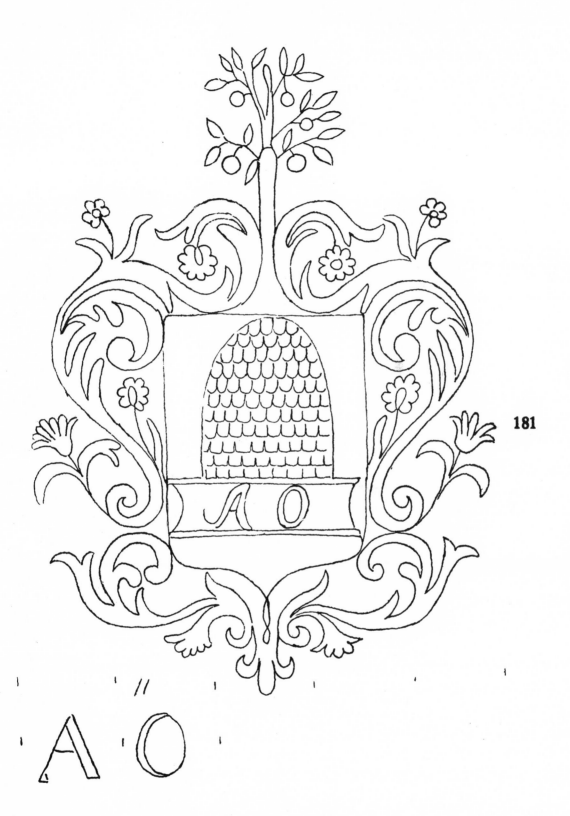

181

182

VanGelder

[CLVIII]

183

184

C&I HONIG

185

G & H

ELEPHANT

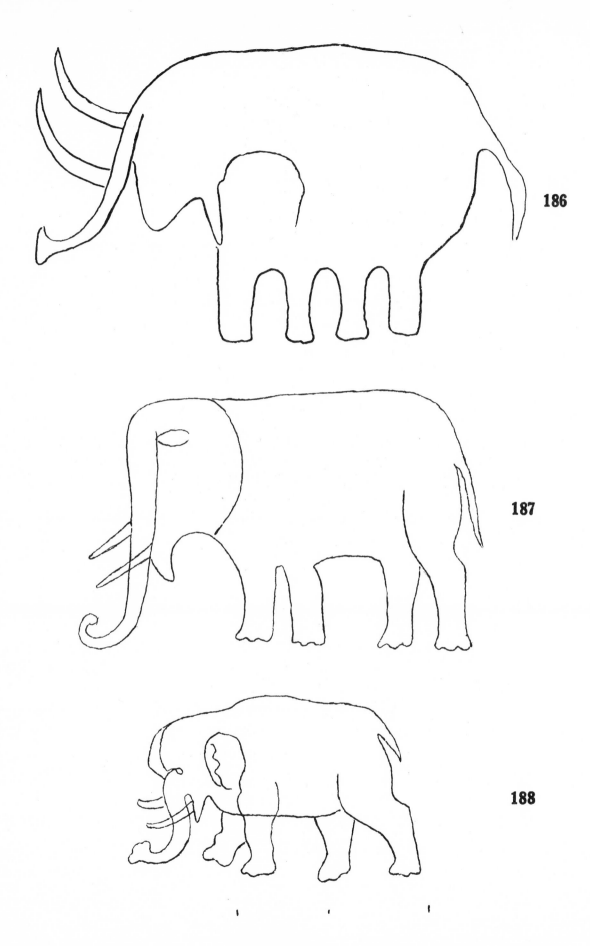

186

187

188

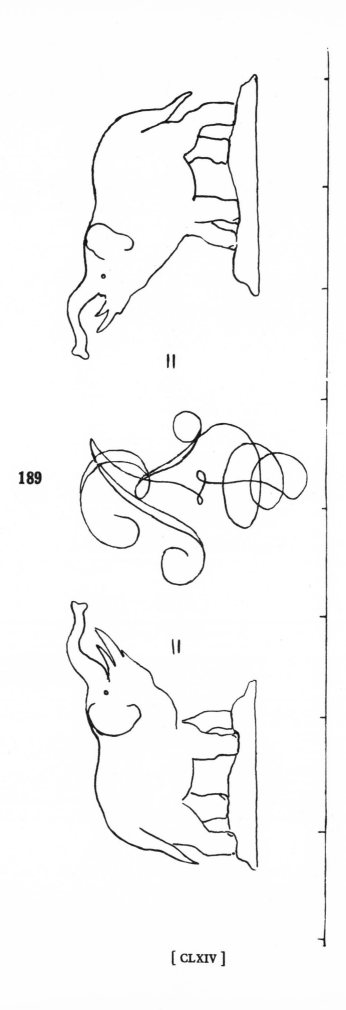

189

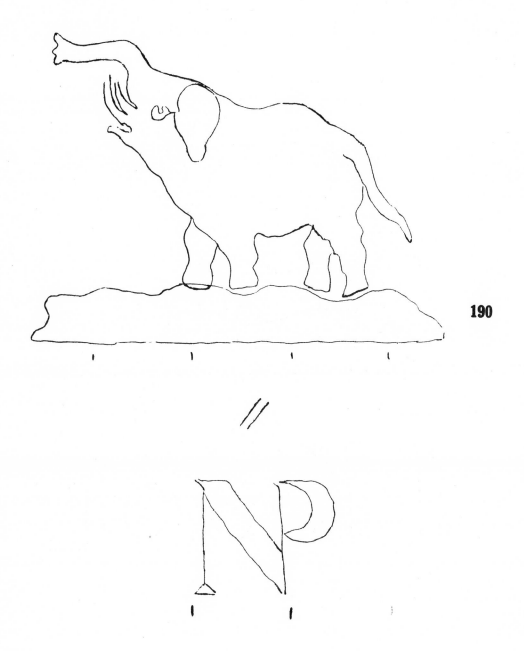

190

191

J K O O L

MISCELLANEOUS MILL MARKS

192

VANDER LEY

[CLXIX]

193

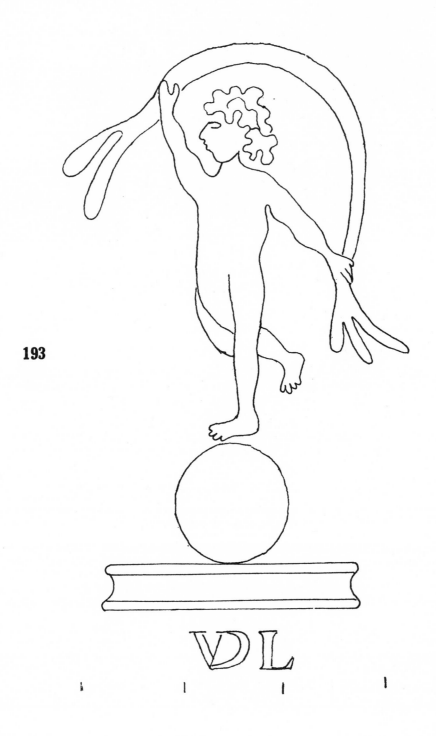

VL

194

HOLLAND   195

JHONIG

[CLXXI]

196

197

J KOOL

198 *Jan Kool & Cᵒ.*

199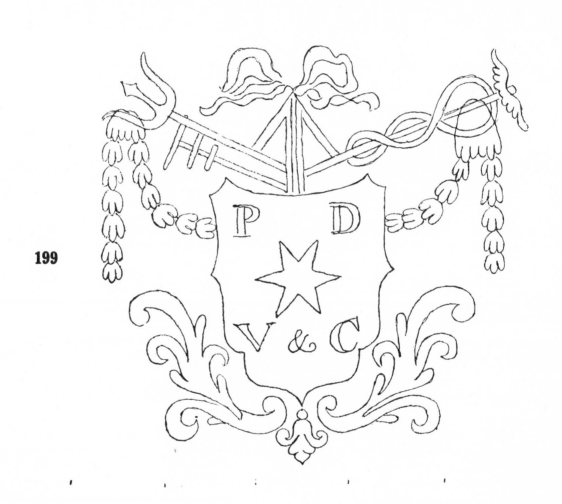

200

W. G. v. d Sande

201

D SEBILLE & WEND

WRAPPERS OR LABELS FOR
REAMS OF PAPER

202

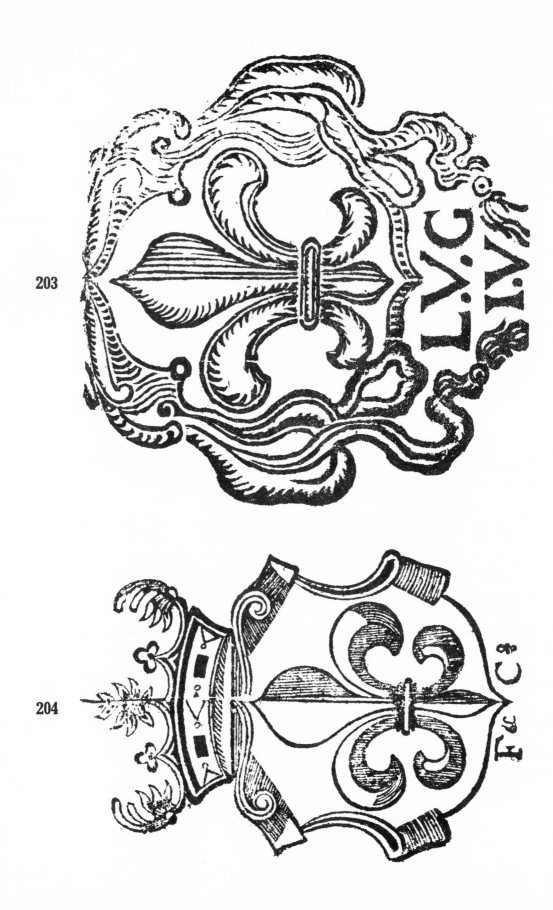

203

204

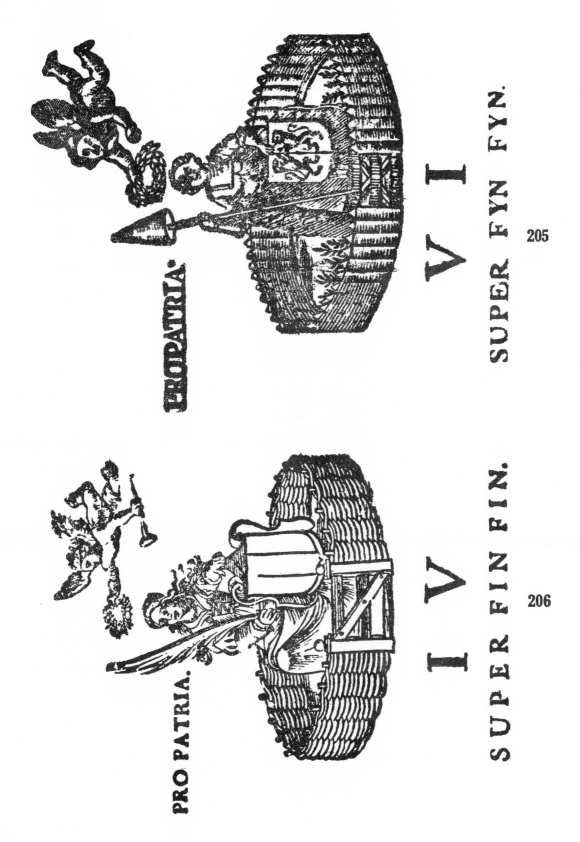

PRO PATRIA.

PRO PATRIA.

V I

SUPER FYN FYN. 205

I V

SUPER FIN FIN. 206

207

EENDRAGT. MAAKT MAGT.

208

FYN PAPIER.

VAN GELDER.

209

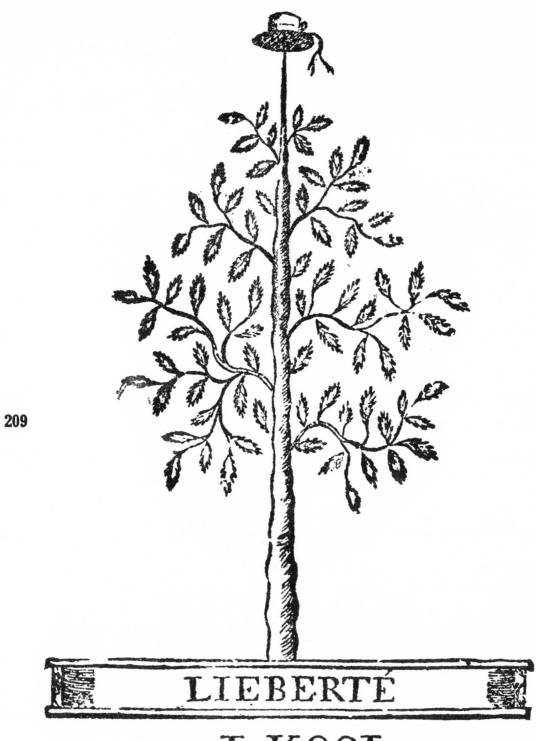

LIEBERTÉ

J. KOOL
FABRIQUER

[CLXXXIV]

ARMS OF ENGLAND

210

211

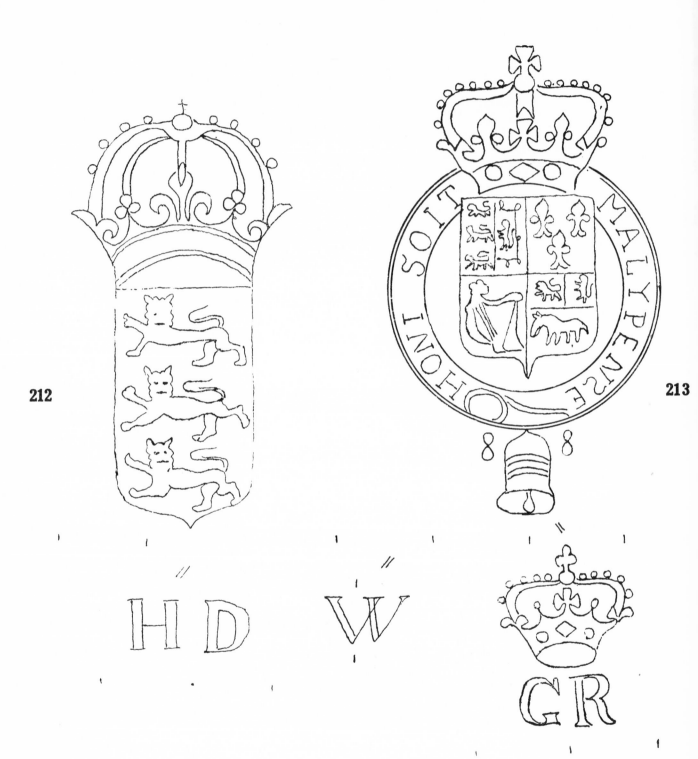

212

213

214

215

216

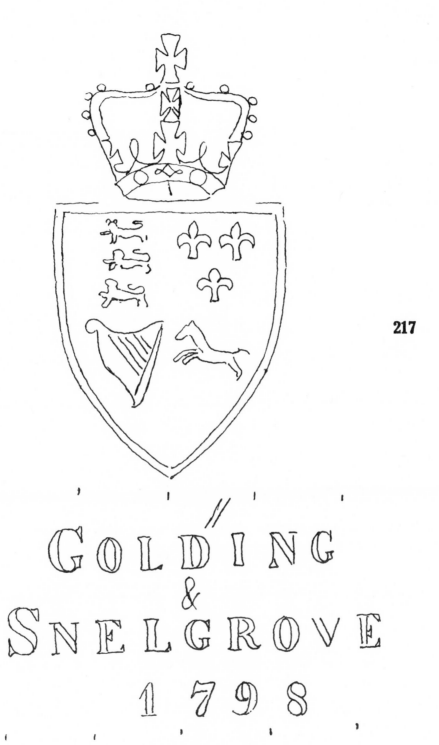

217

GOLDING
&
SNELGROVE
1798

218

BRITTANNIA

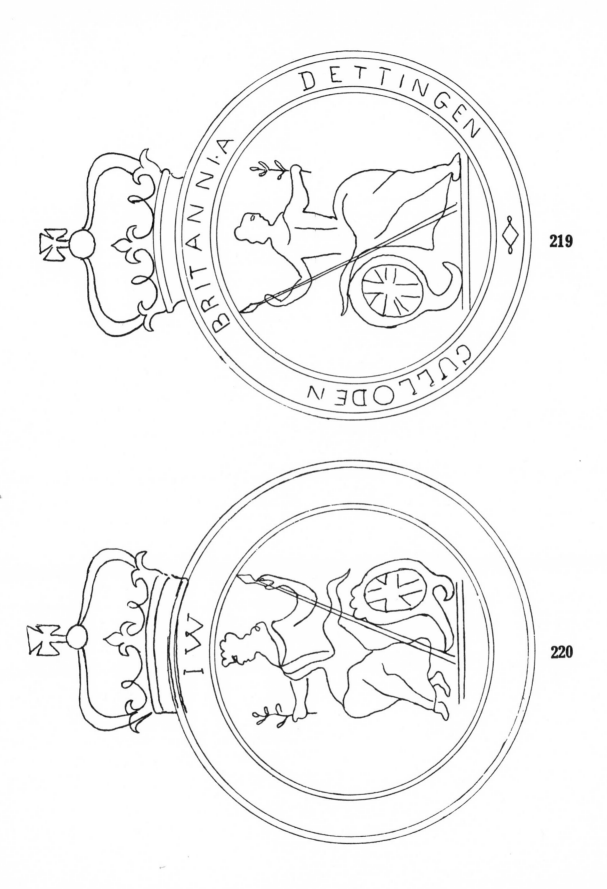

219

220

221

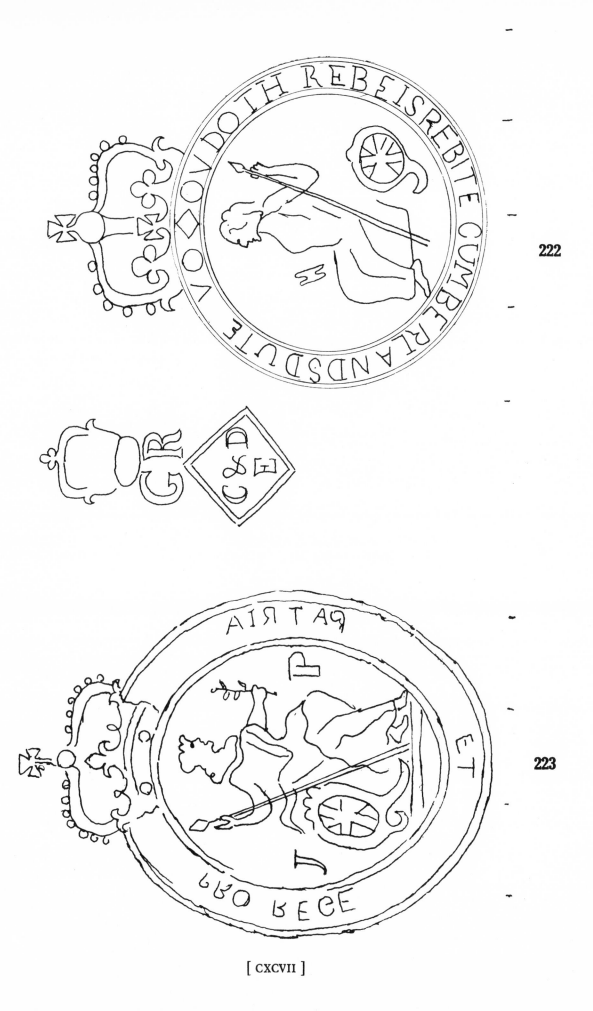

222

223

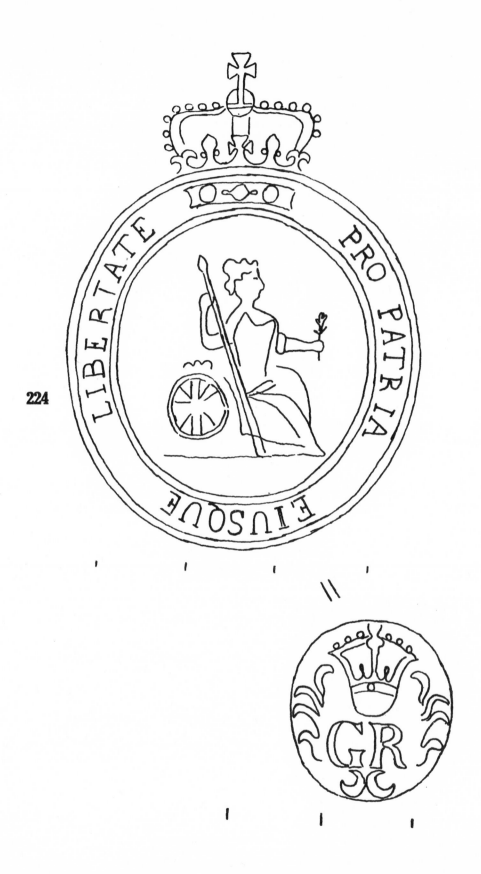

224

225

226

LVG

227

Countermark to left

L V G

[CCI]

228

229

230

231

//

CURTEIS & SON'S

[CCIV]

232

233

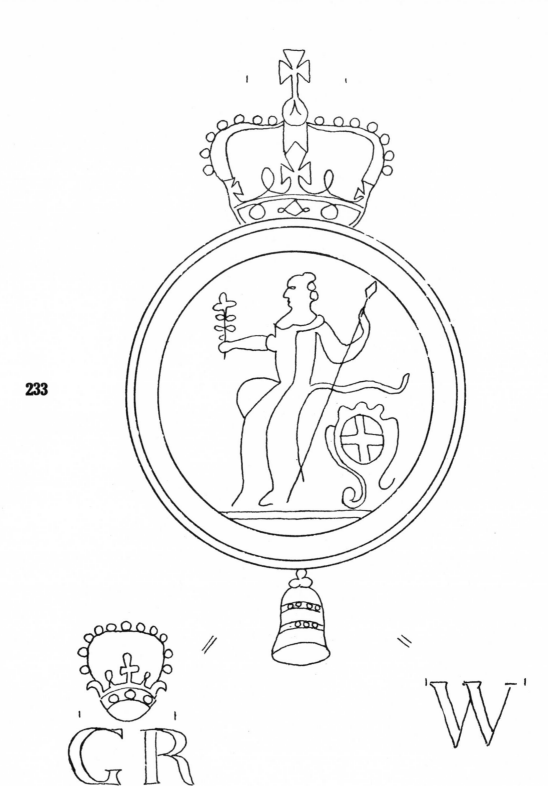

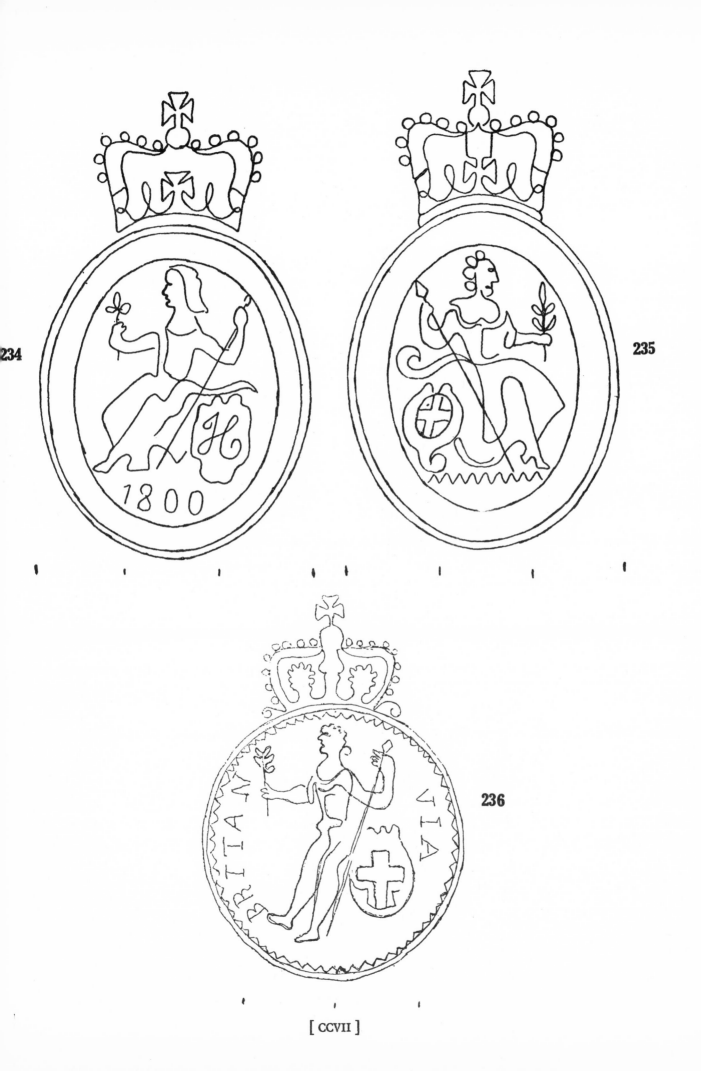

234

235

236

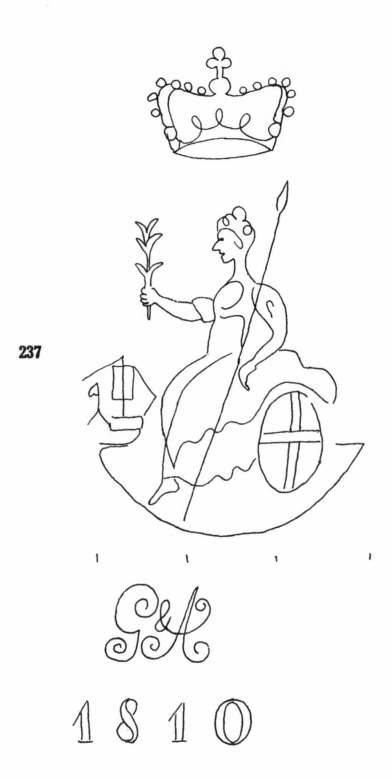

237

238

LONDON COAT-OF-ARMS

239

240

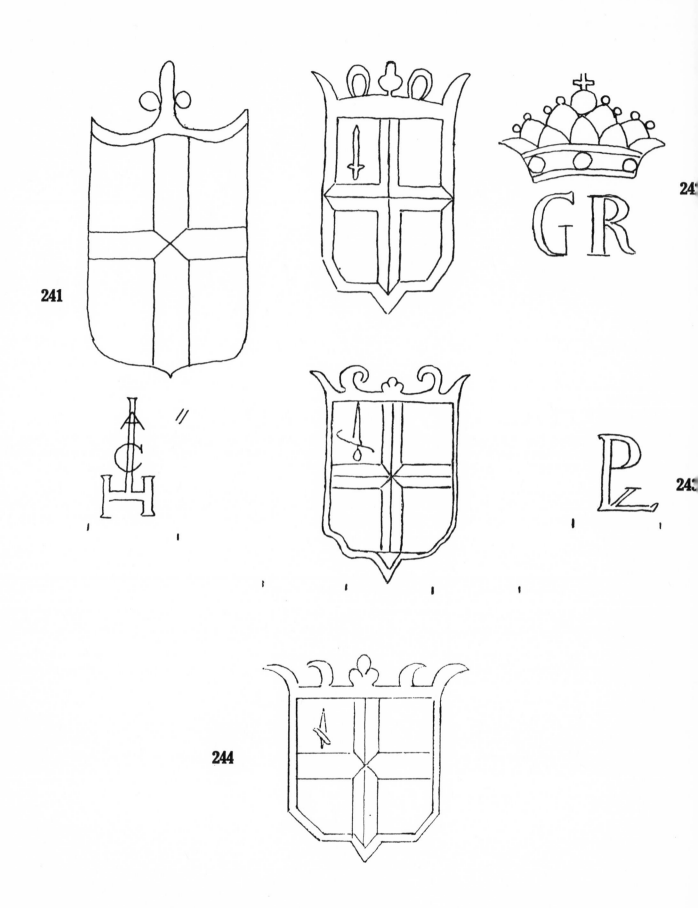

241

242

243

244

ROYAL CIPHERS, AND BELL

245

246

Watermarks in paper.

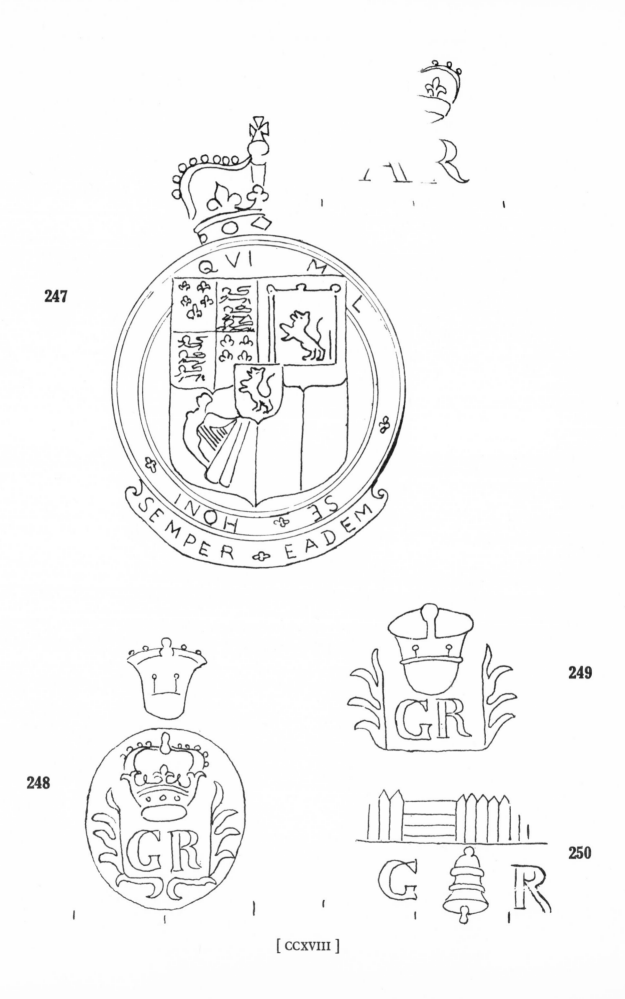

247

249

248

250

251

252

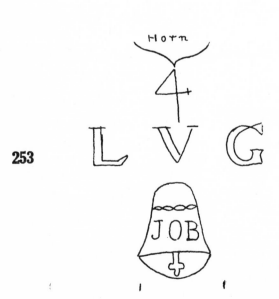

253

254

255

//

D&C BLAUW

256

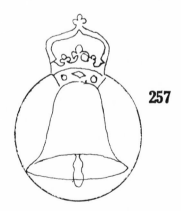

257

FRANCE, HOLLAND, ENGLAND, ETC.
COATS-OF-ARMS

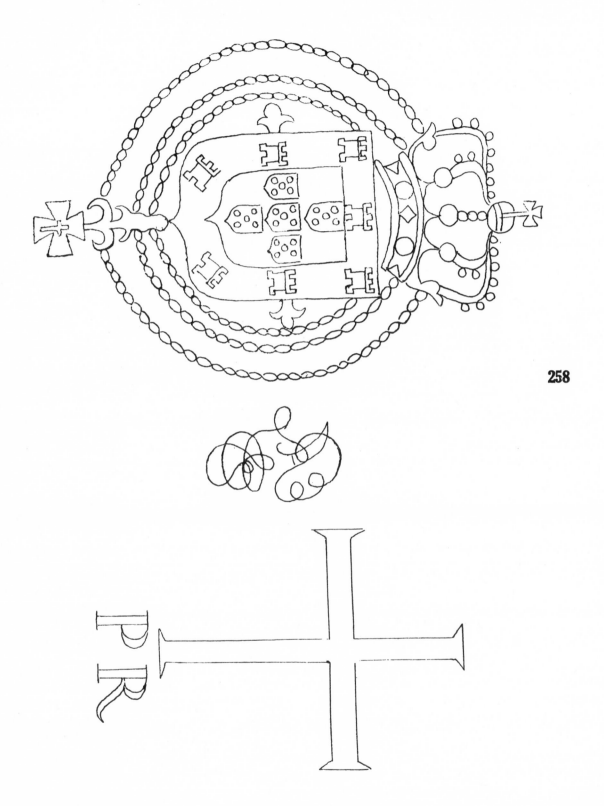

258

259

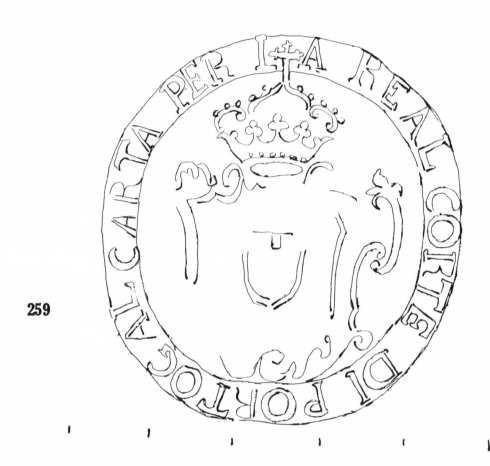

POLLERA

[CCXXIV]

260

[CCXXV]

261

262

263

A M A

[CCXXVIII]

264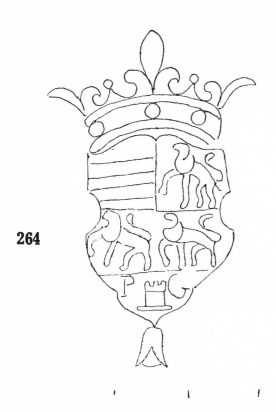

 **265**

266

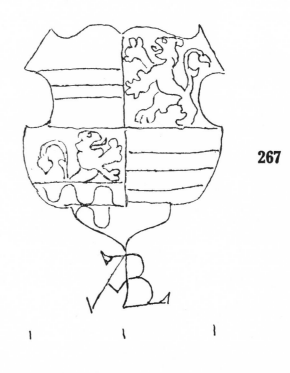 **267**

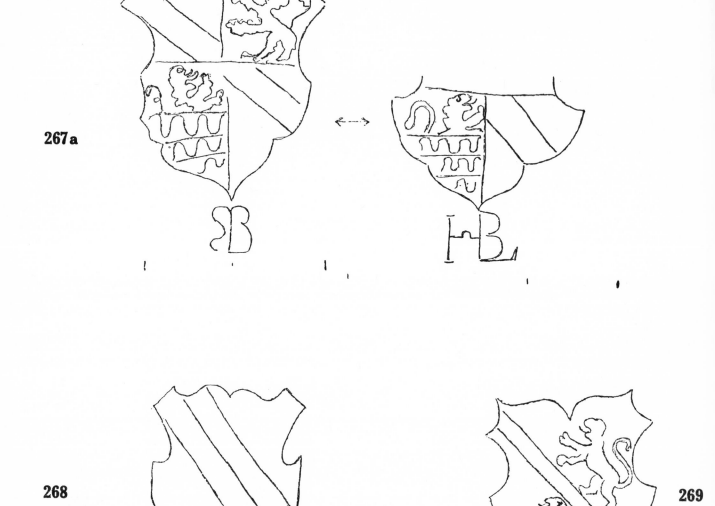

267a

268

269

270

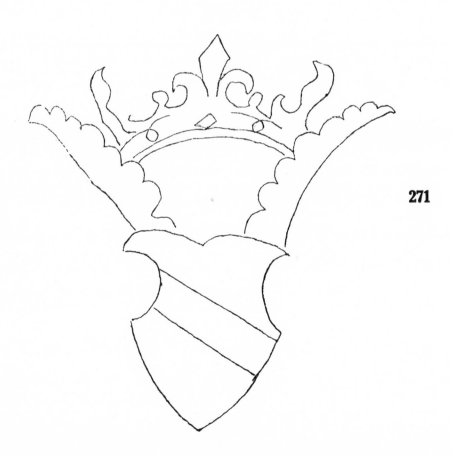

271

272

273

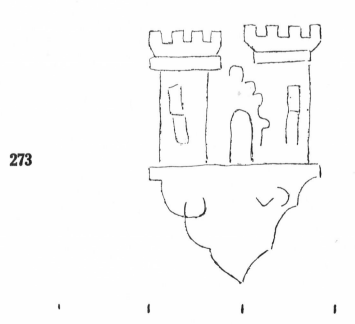

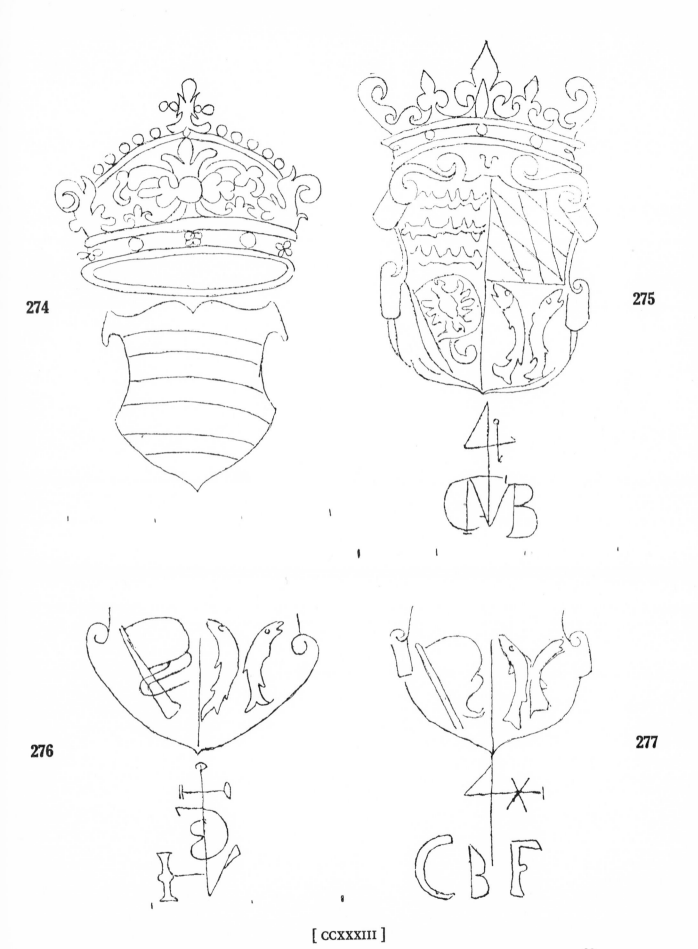

274

275

276

277

Watermarks in paper.

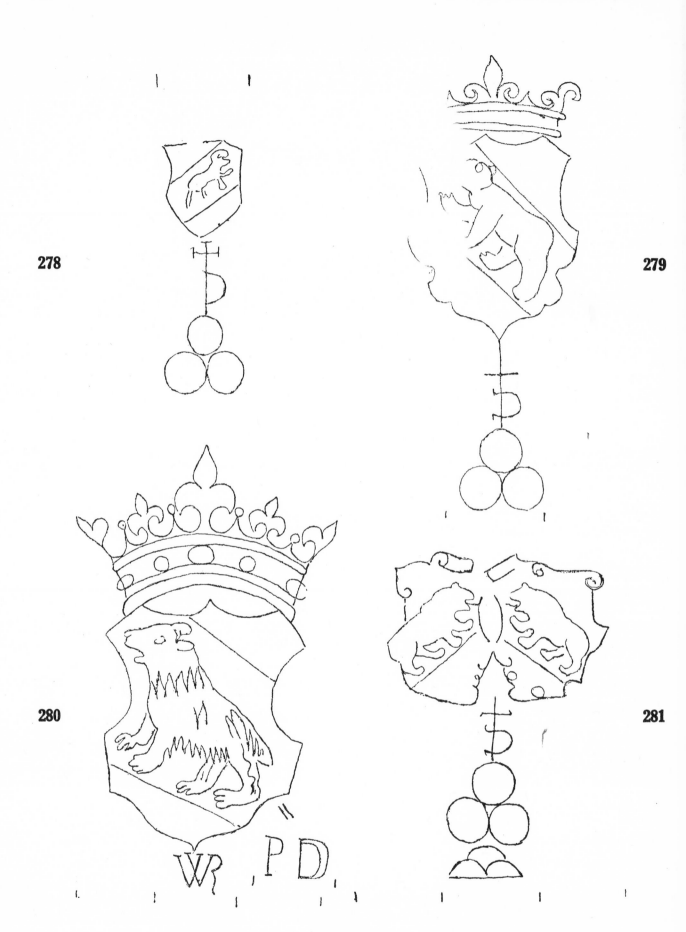

278

279

280

281

WR PD

282

283

284

285

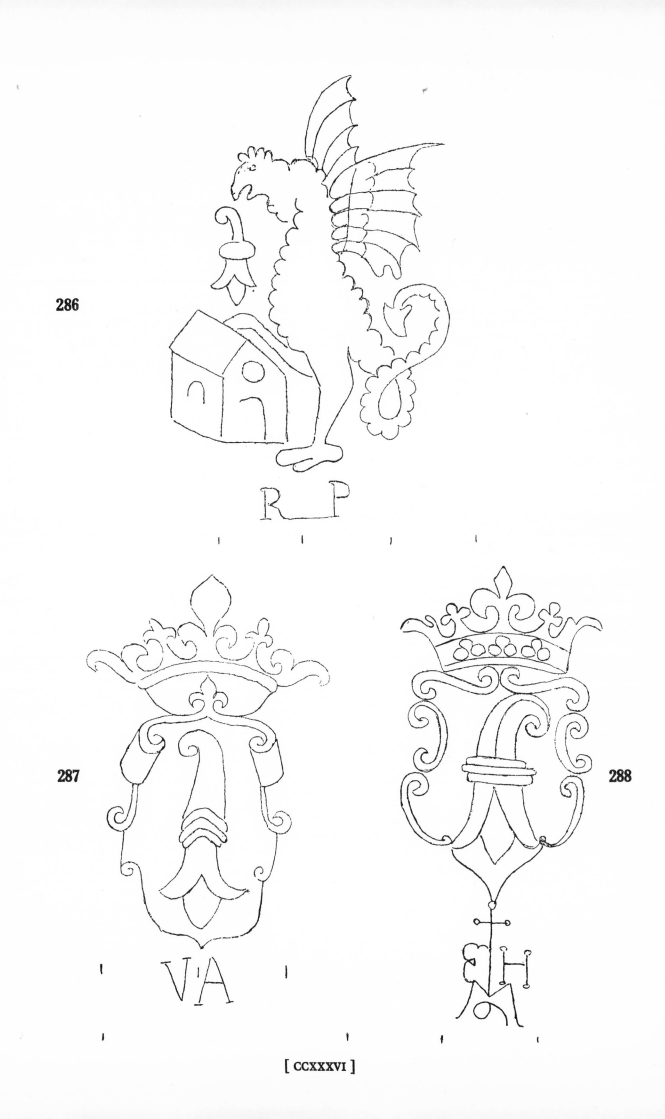

286

287 288

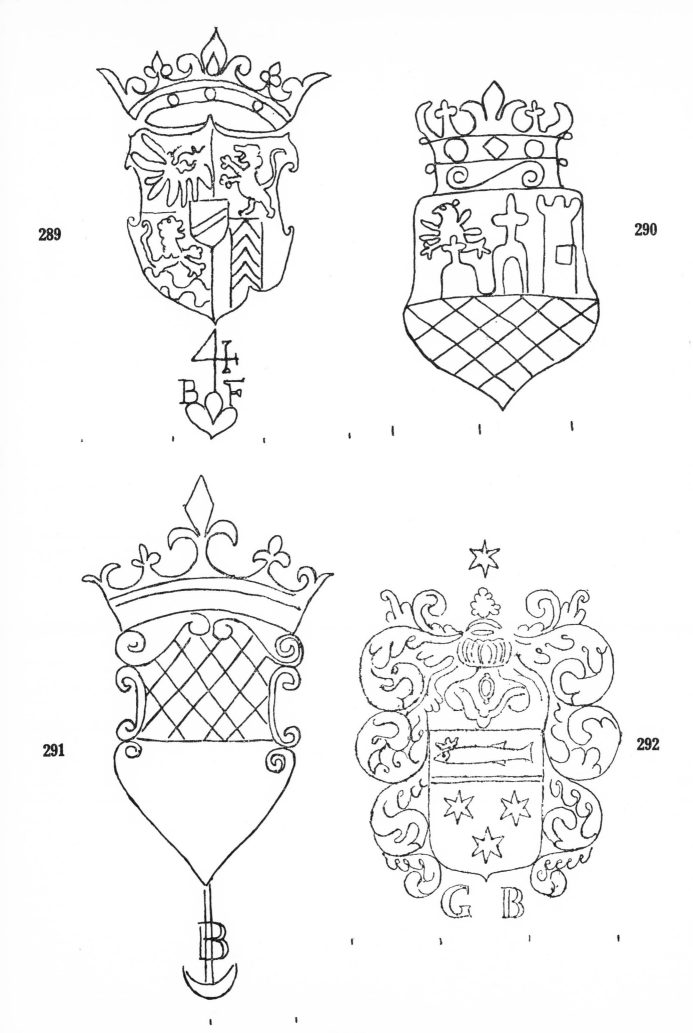

289

290

291

292

293 294

295 296

297

298

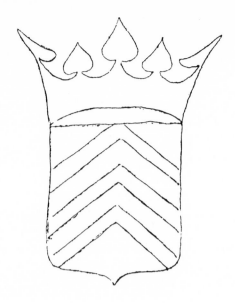

299

300

PAPIER F·FAICT
G GAMONTIGNA
CHERAN·TE "

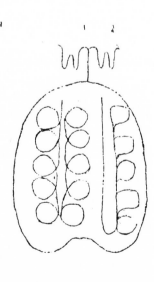

301

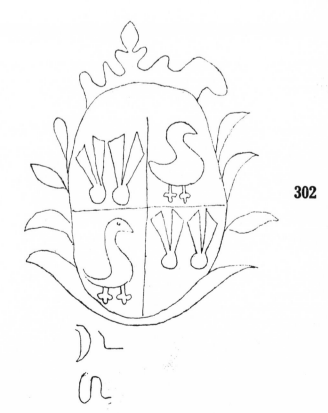

302

Watermarks in paper.

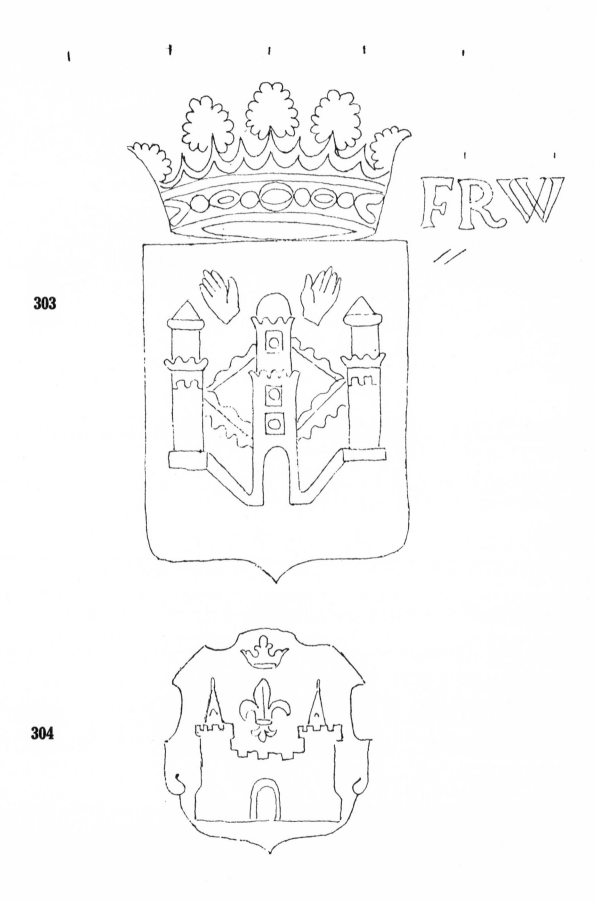

303

304

FRW

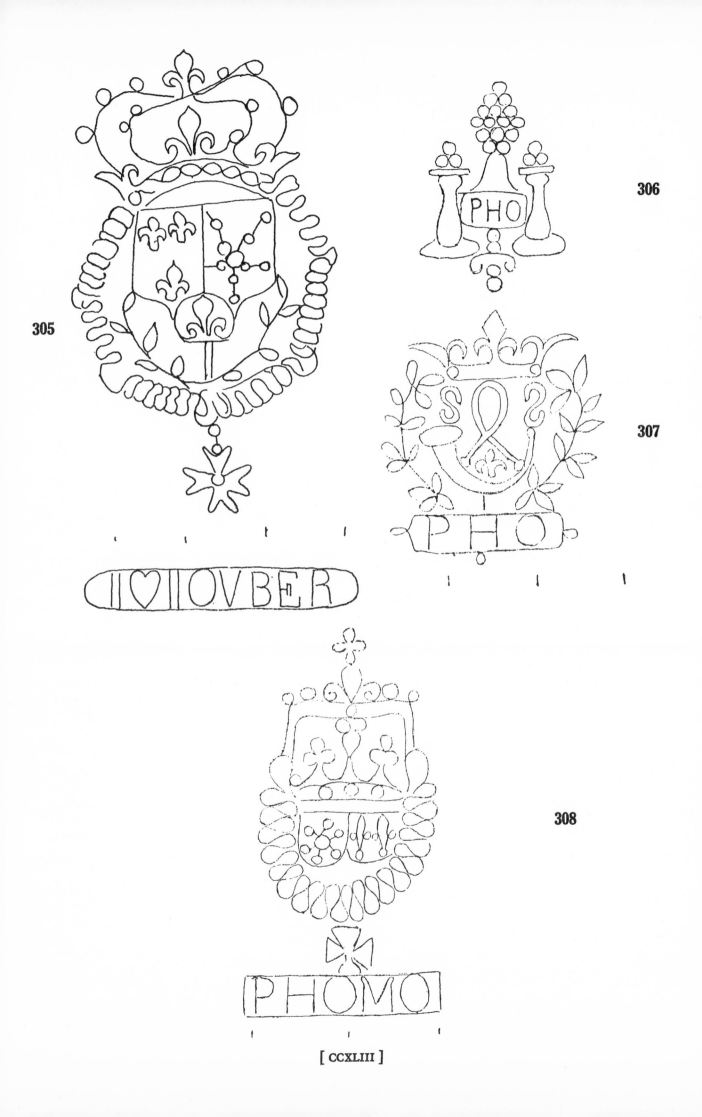

305

306

307

308

309

FABRICA   NOVA

310

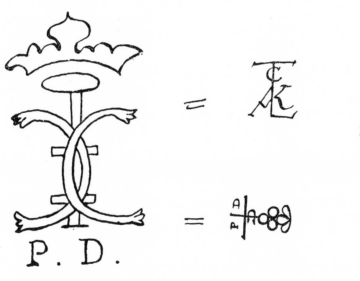

311

P. D.

312

HORN

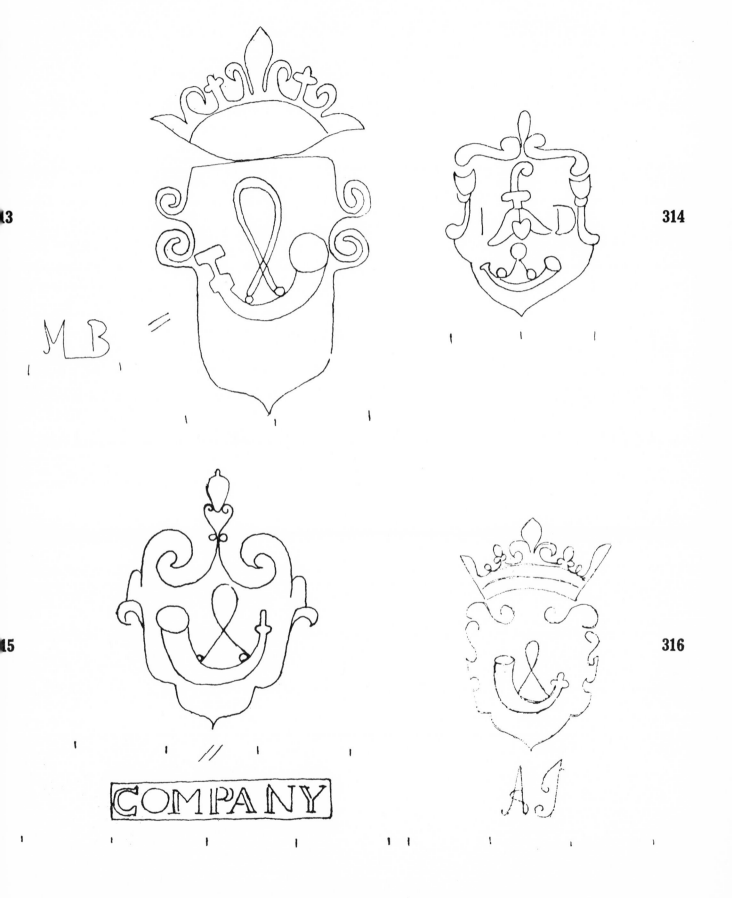

313

314

315

316

MB

COMPANY

AJ

Watermarks in paper.

317

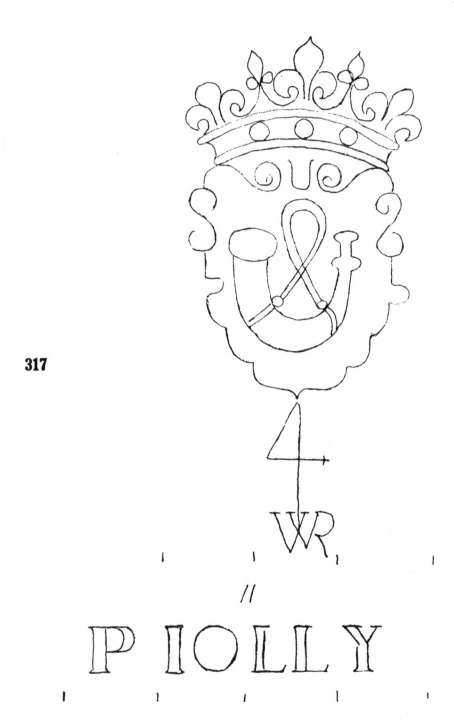

P IOLLY

318

L V Gᴇʀʀᴇᴠɪɴᴋ

319

ɪᴠG

320

R&W STIRLING

321

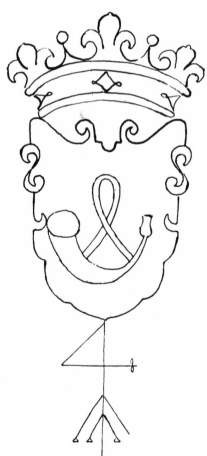

VANDER LEY.

JHONIG
&
ZOONEN

322

GR

323

324

J W HATMAN

325

VAN DER LEY

326

N.°PANNEKOEK

327

328

M

329

D & C Blauw

330

B & B

331

GR /. KETEL. & WASSEN ERGII.

[CCLVIII]

POSTILION

332

333

334

FOOLSCAP

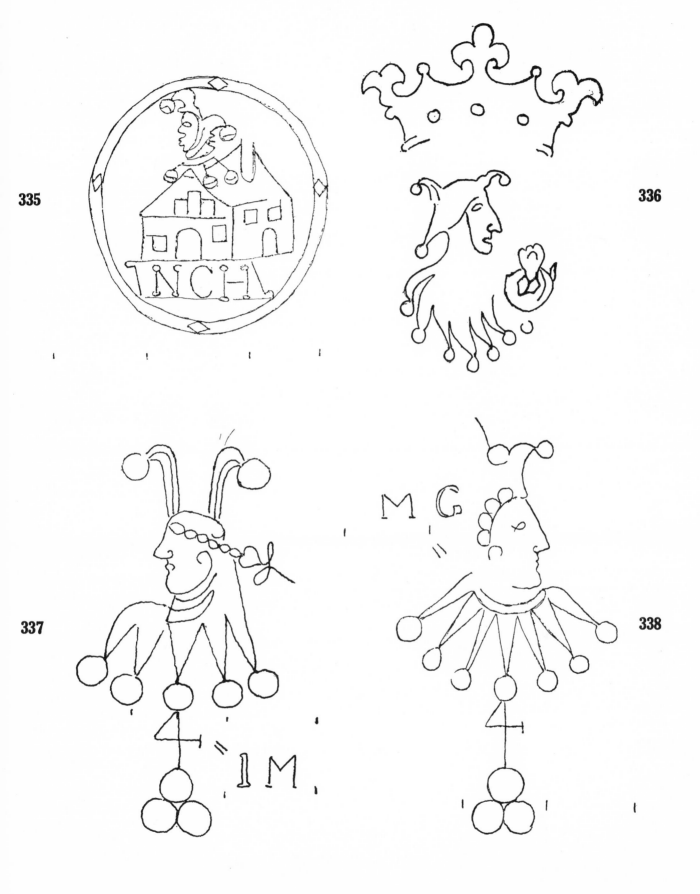

335

336

337

338

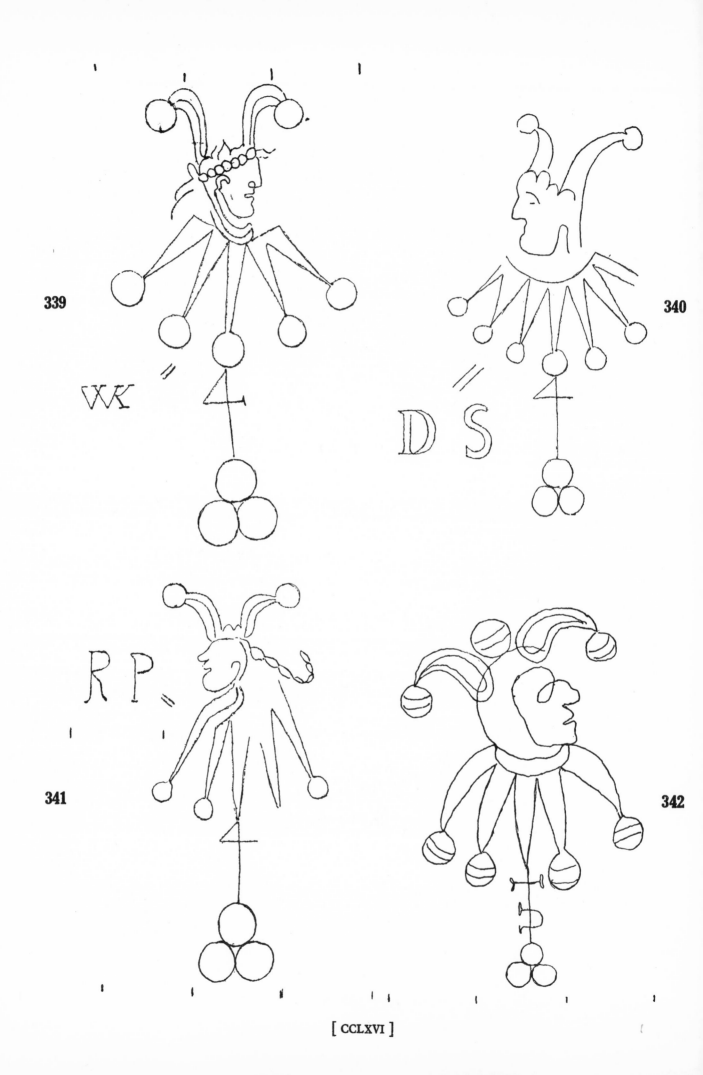

339

340

WK

RP.

DS

341

342

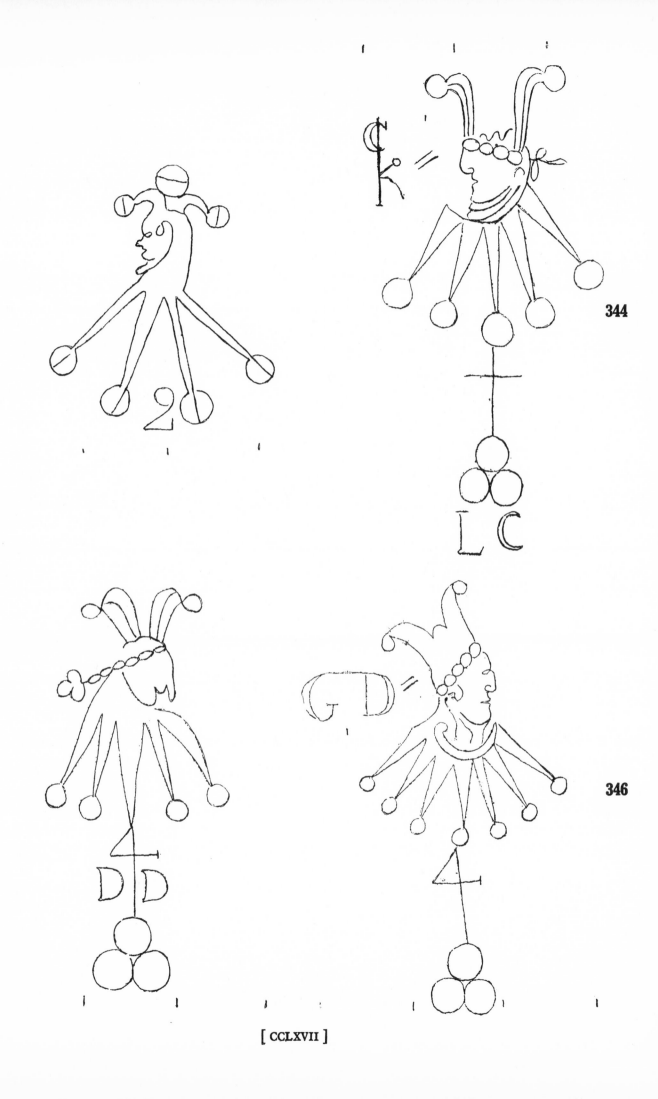

343

344

345

346

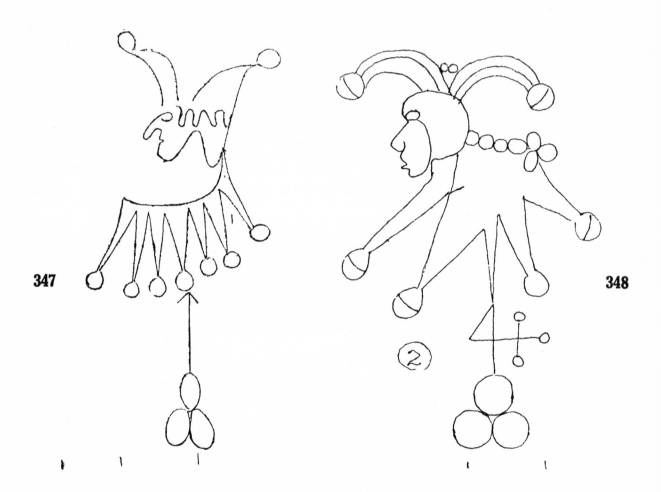

347

348

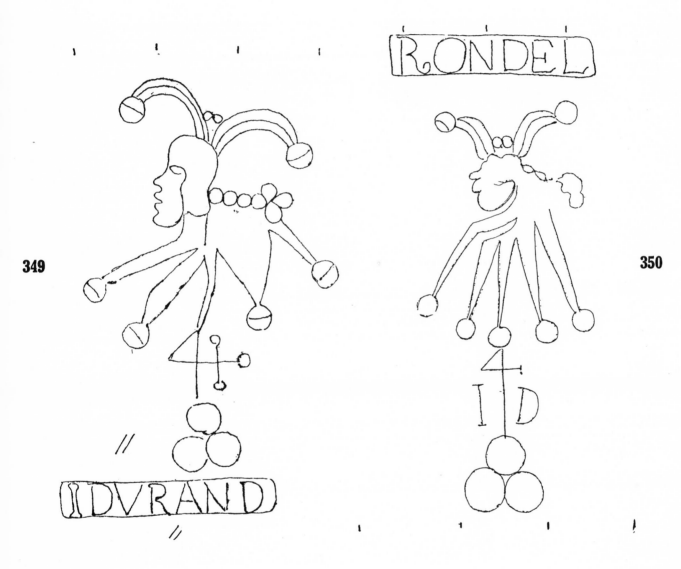

349

350

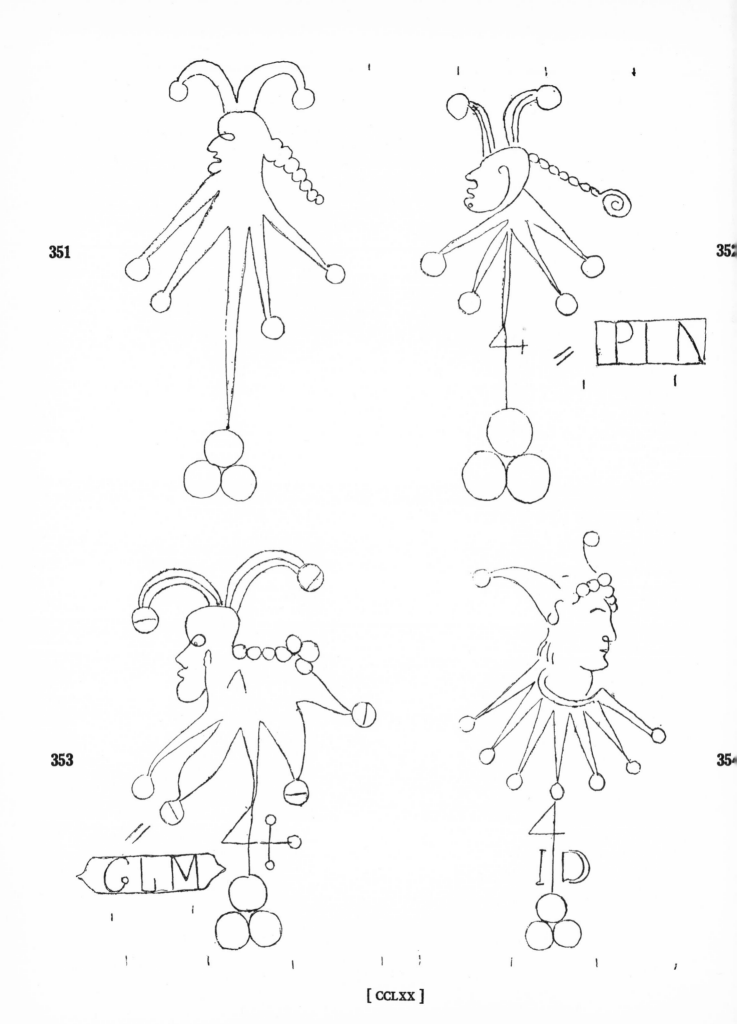

351

352

353

354

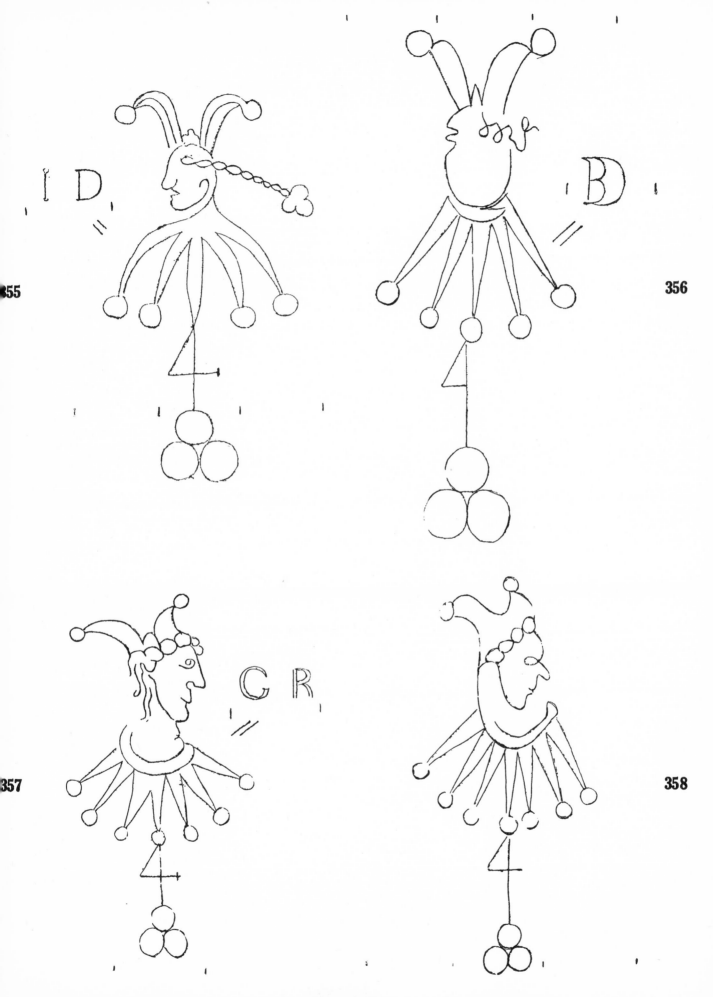

355

356

357

358

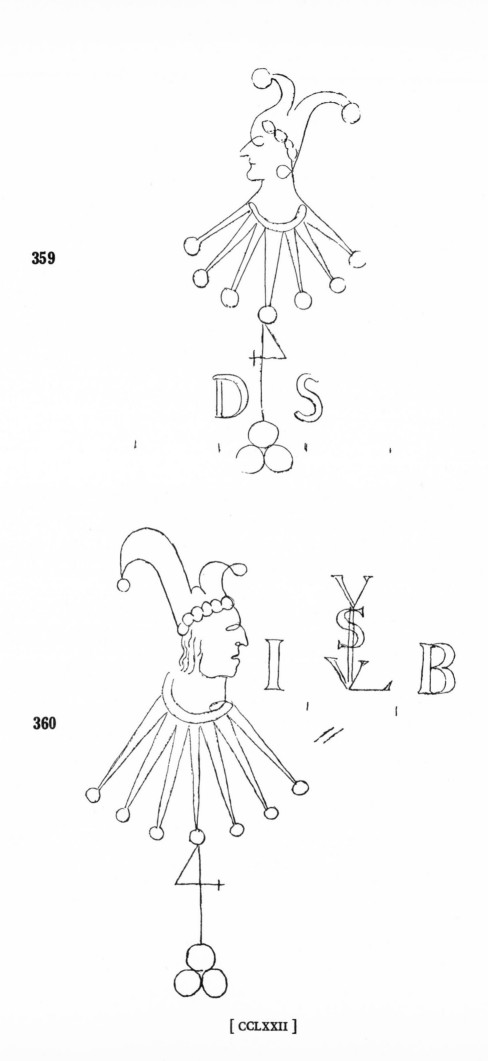

359

360

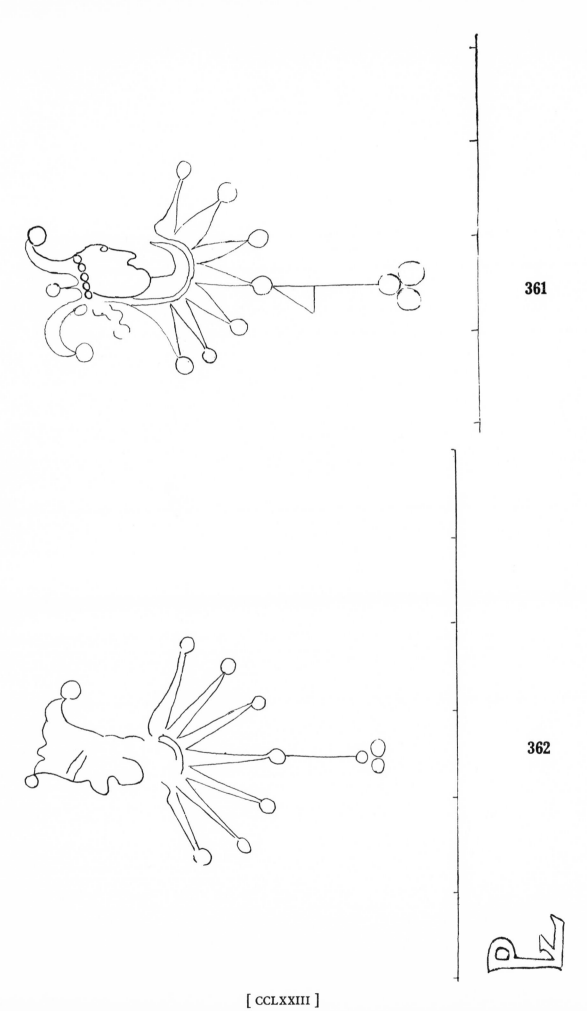

361

362

[CCLXXIII]

363

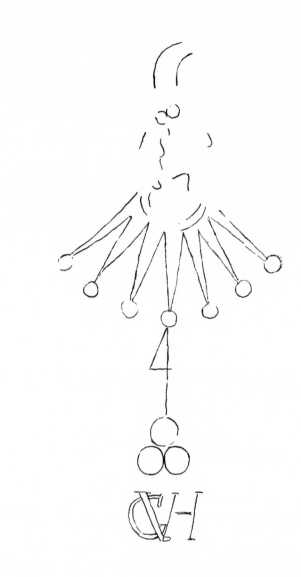

I VILLEDARY

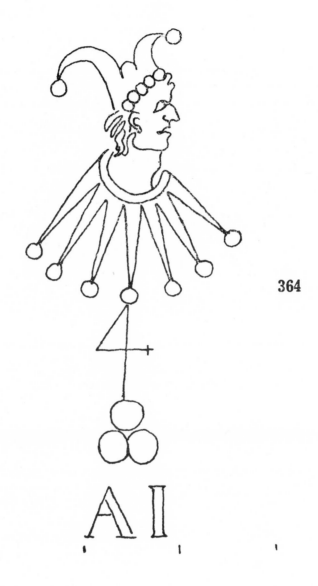

364

AI

365

366

PAPIER FAIT AV
MOVLIN DE S.MICHEL
PAR M.FSTIENNE
TOVZEAV

367

Fyne NarrenCap

LILIES

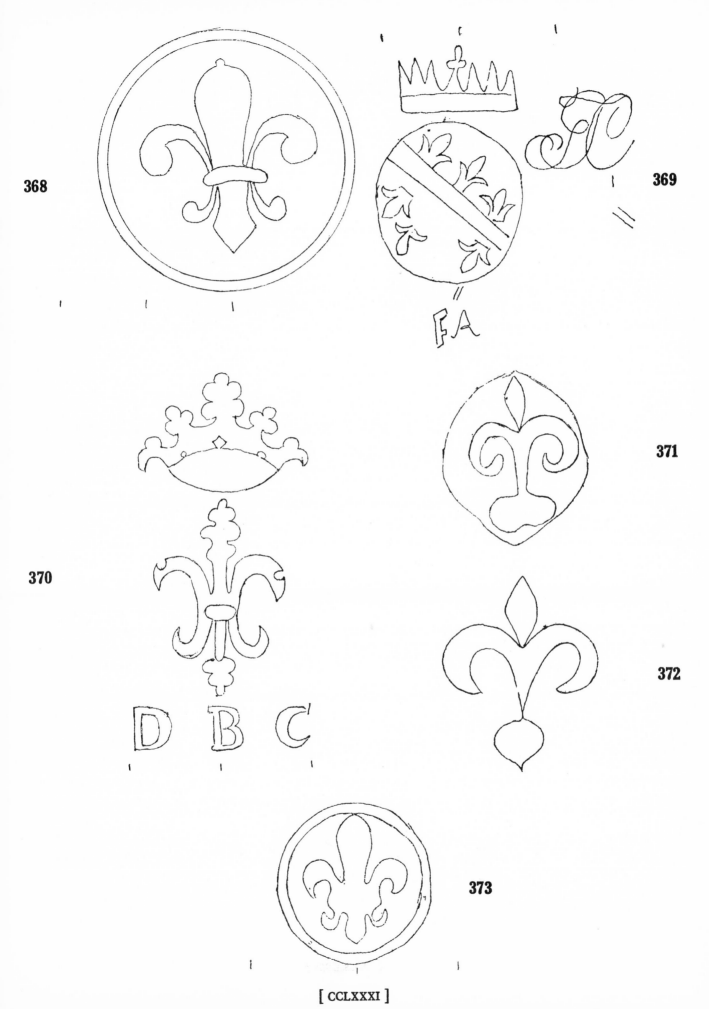

368

369

371

370

372

373

[CCLXXXI]

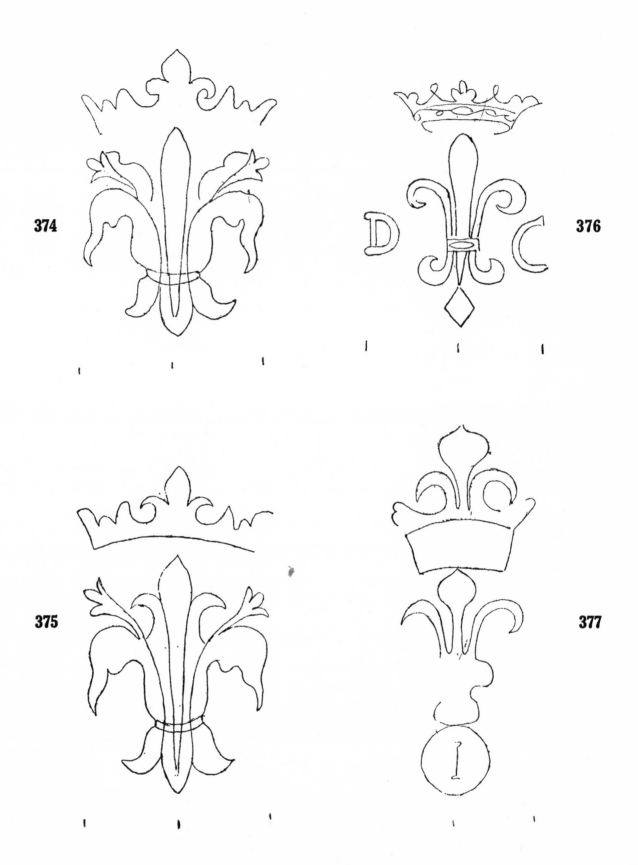

374

376

375

377

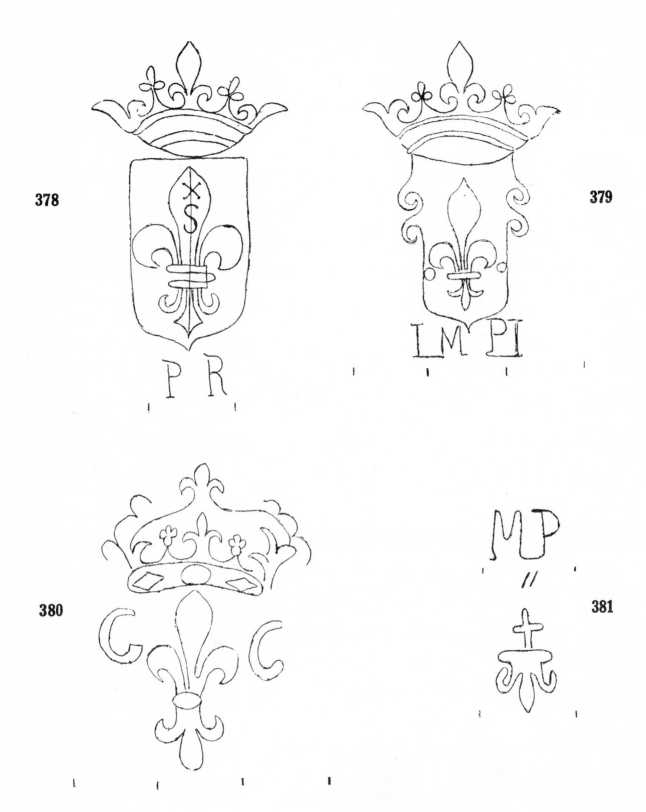

378

379

380

381

382

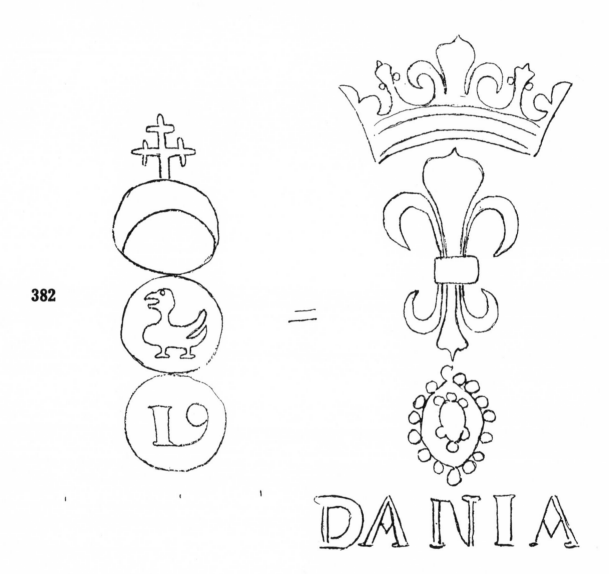

DANIA

383

NICOLO POLERI

384

S B PATRONE
 P

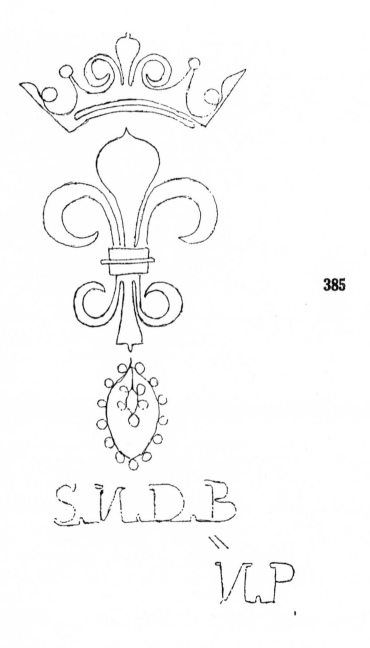

385

S.M.D.B

V.P.

386

P
POYLEVE
A LYMOGE

P MR LEIE
A VITRÉ 1633

L
XIII

387

388

389

390

391 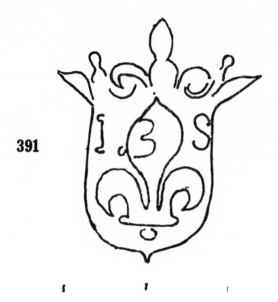 392

393

394

395

396

DURHAM WINCHCOMBE
GLOUCESTER SHIRE

P IONAS

FIN ANGOUMOIS

397

D ∝ B

F D'ANGOUMOIS

398

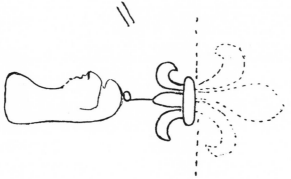

399

STRASBURG LILY

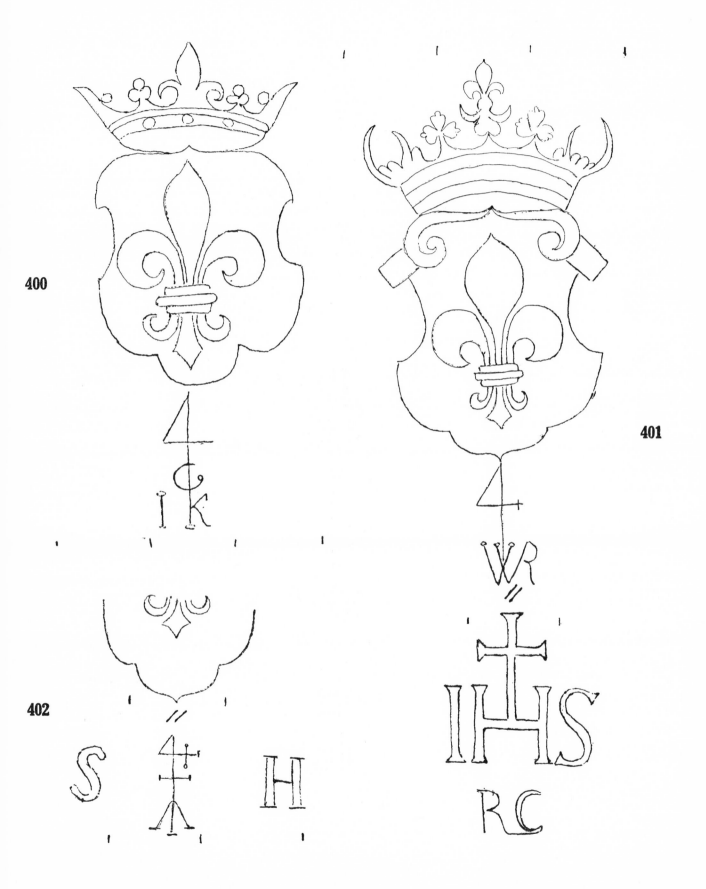

400

401

402

Watermarks in paper.

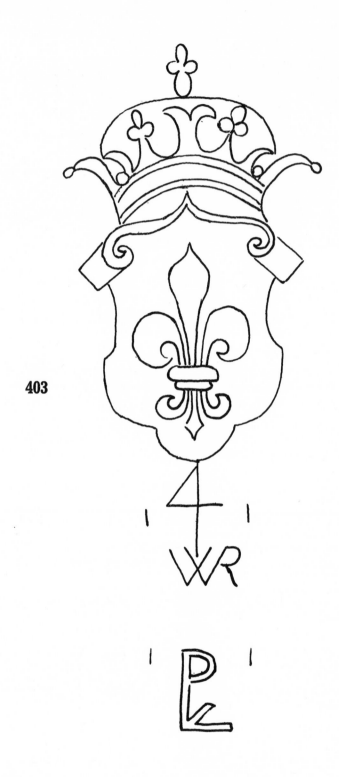

403

VAN DER LEY

404

405

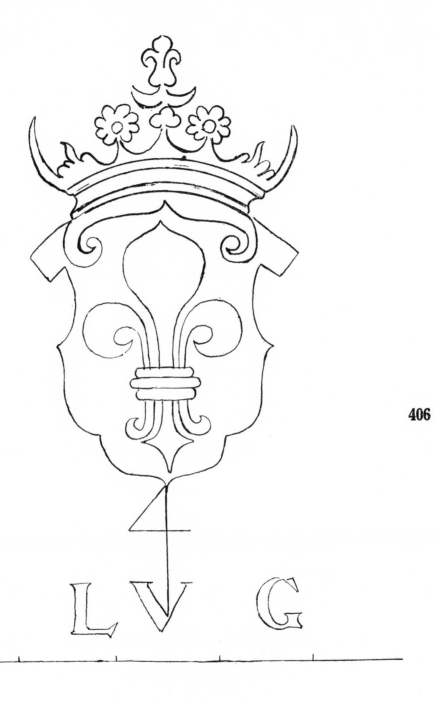

406

LV G

IV

407

I VILLEDARY

408

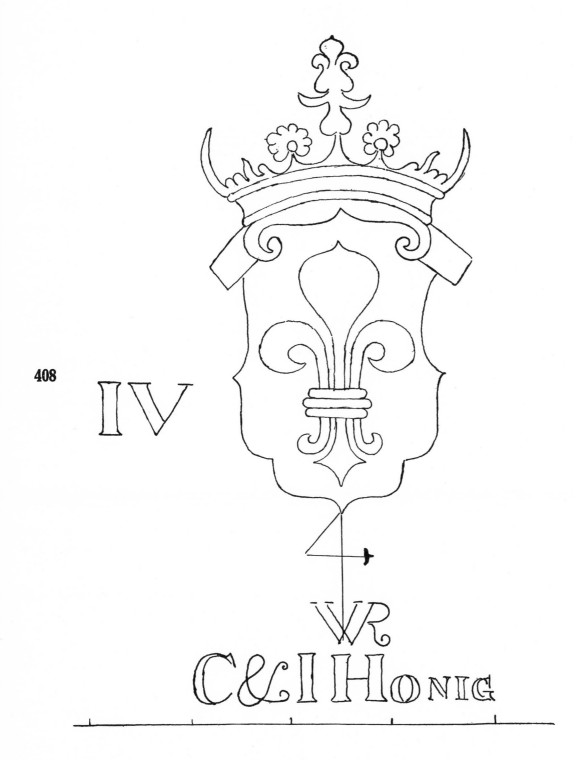

IV

C & I Honig

409

A D R I A A N   R O G G E

I   V I L L E D A R Y

[CCCIV]

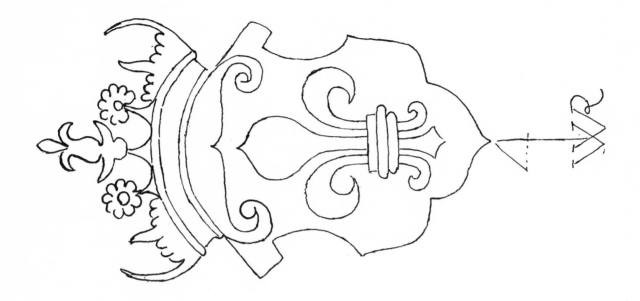

410

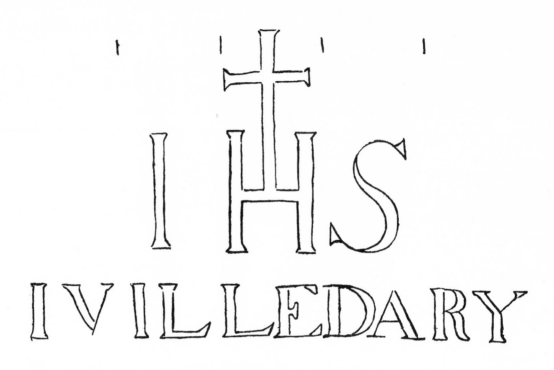

IVILLEDARY

411

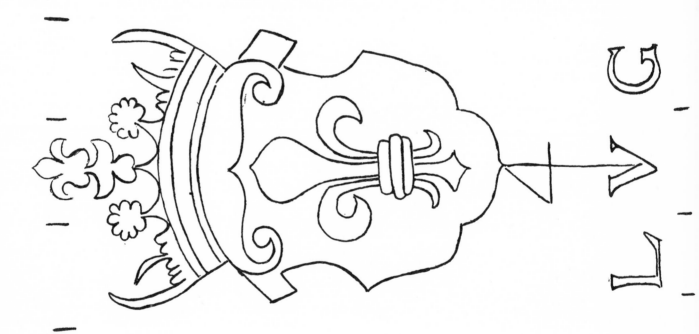

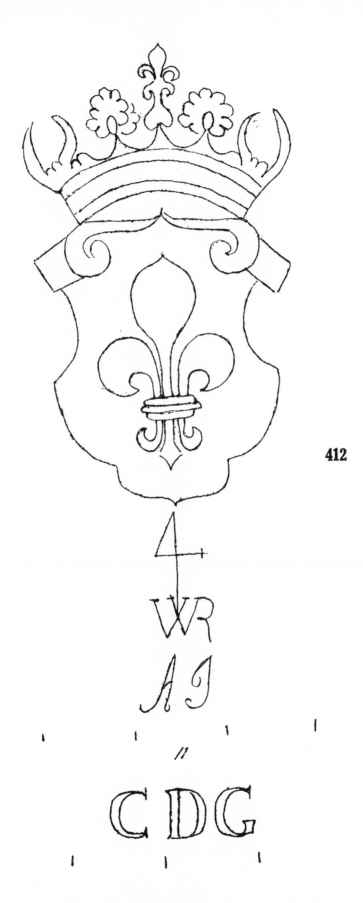

412

413

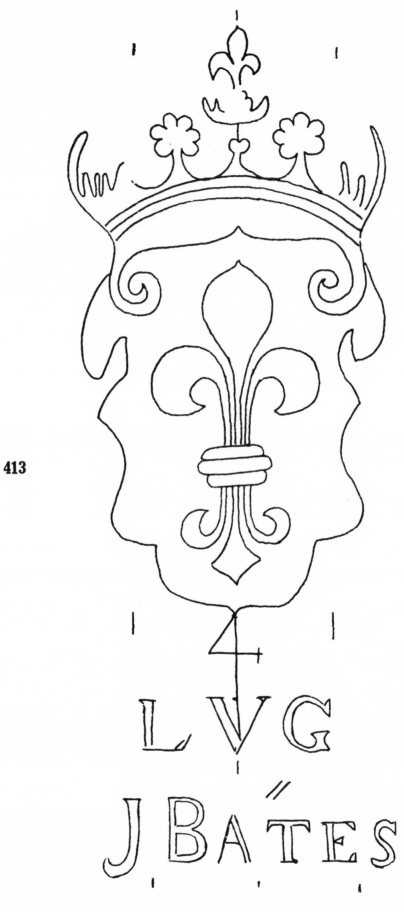

[CCCVIII]

I × PORTAL =

414

L V G

415

J. WHATMAN

KORFF & DE VRIES

416

417

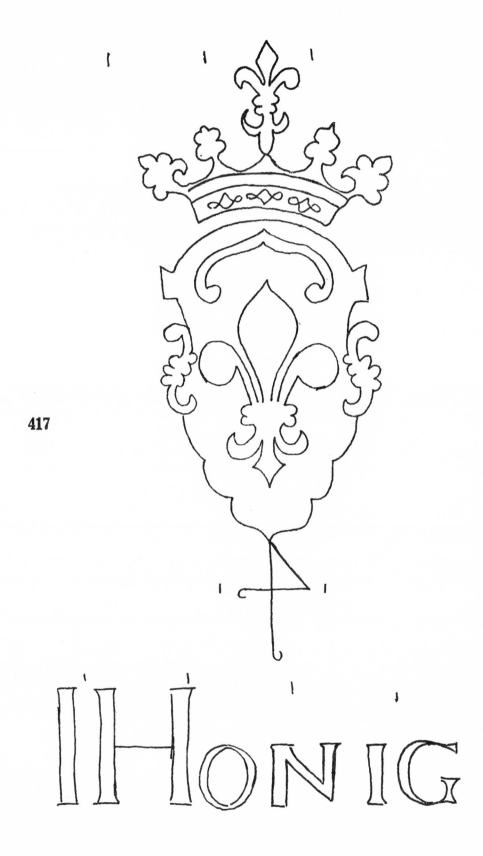

VAN EGMONT

418

Watermarks in paper.

40

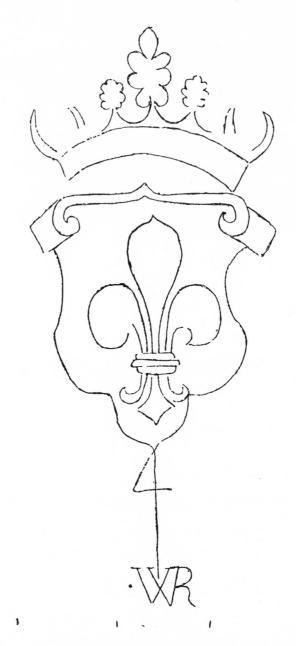

419

·VR

I DVRANDAVS

420

BE AV UA IS

421

J KOOL

422

CH. I. DL & C°

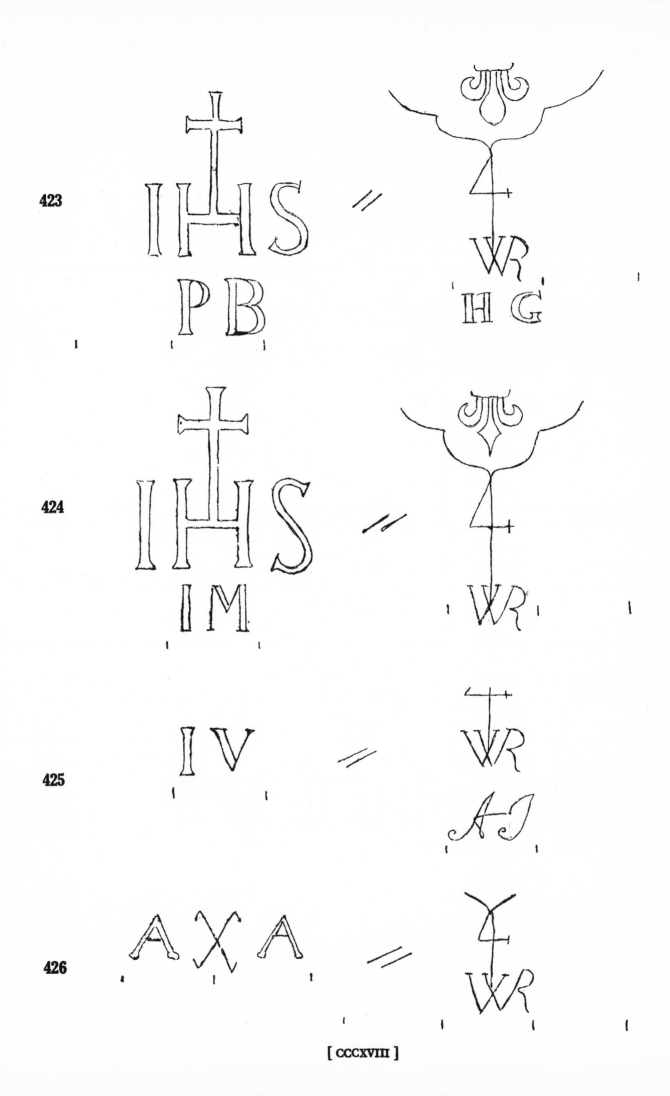

423

424

425

426

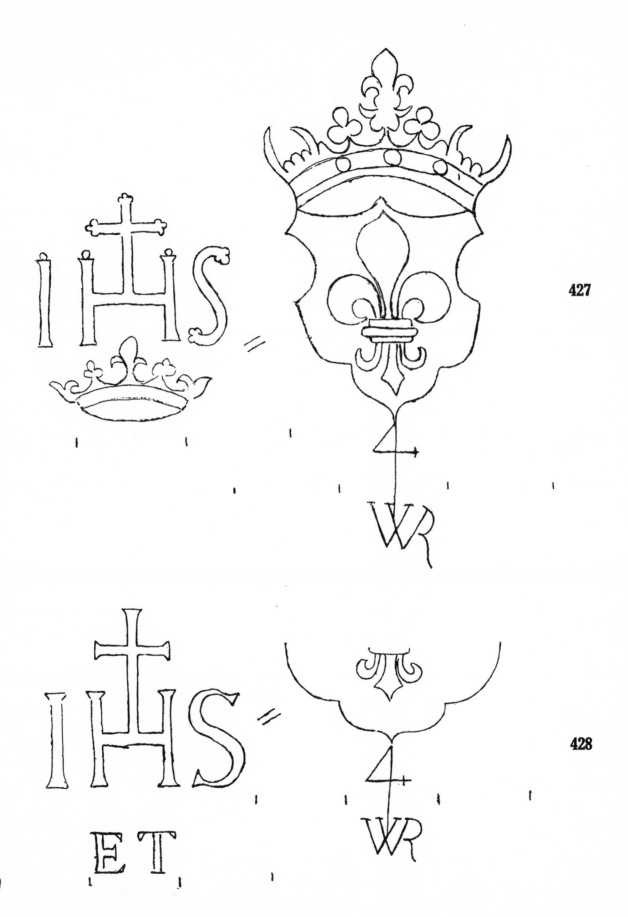

427

428

STRASBURG BEND & LILY

429

C & I HONIG

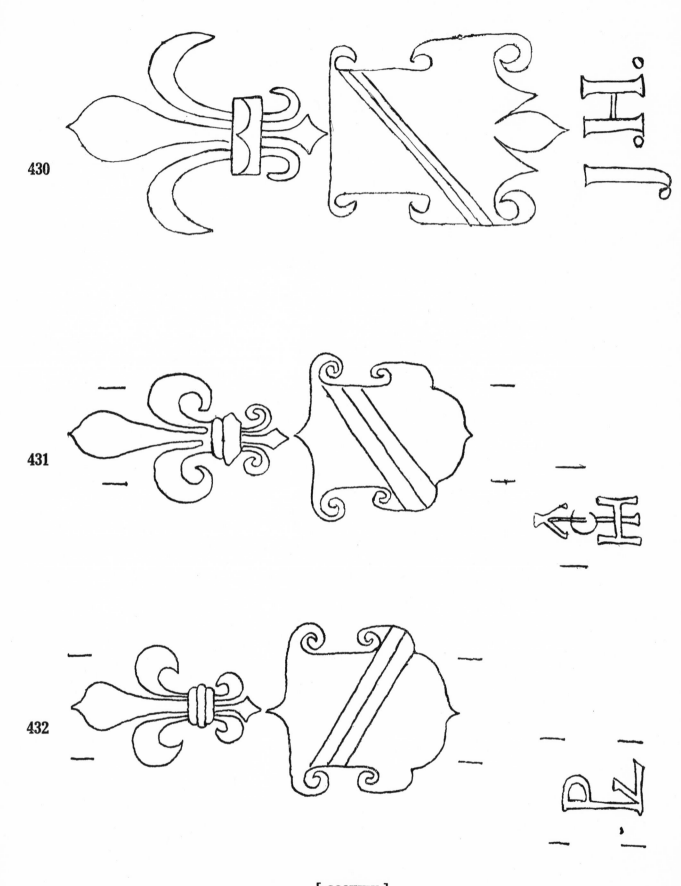

430

J. H.

431

H.

432

J. F.

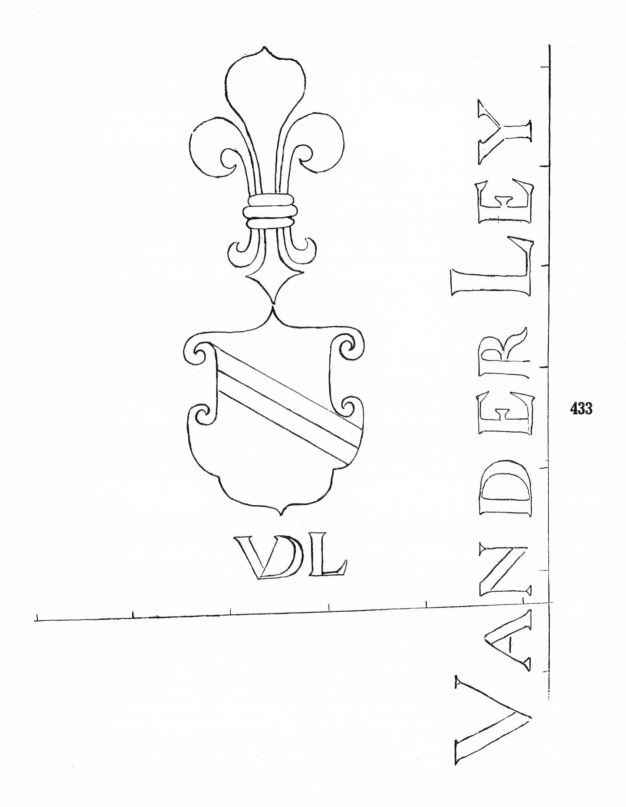

VDL

VAN DER LEY

433

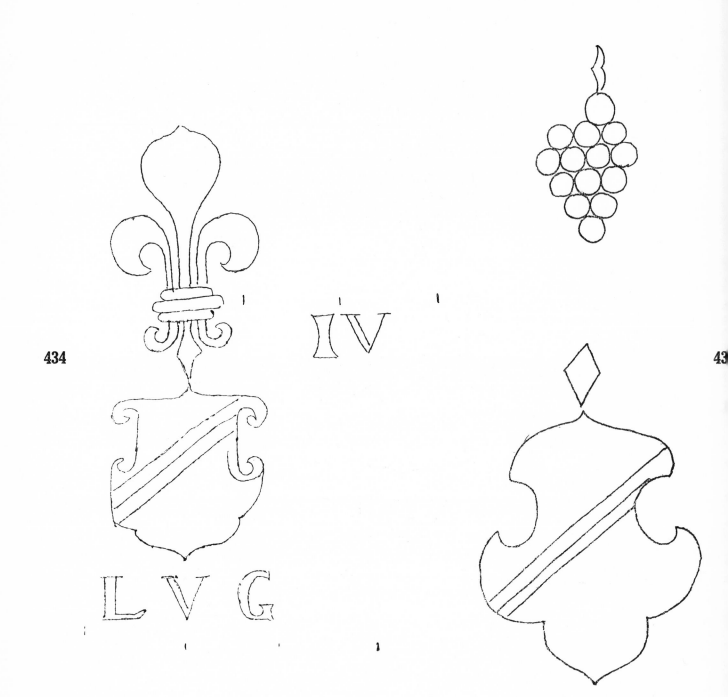

434

43

IV

L V G

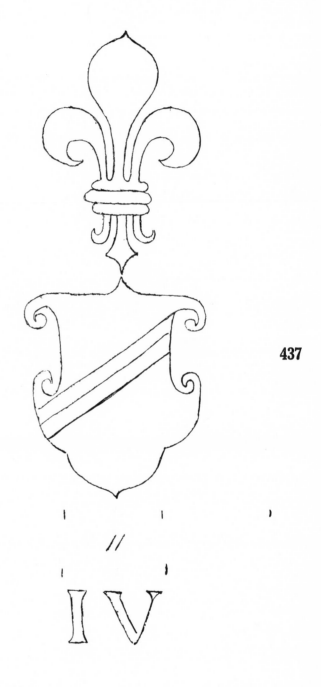

36
437

A D S
IV

[CCCXXVII]

EAGLE

438

439

440

441

442

443

PB

444

PB

//

VG

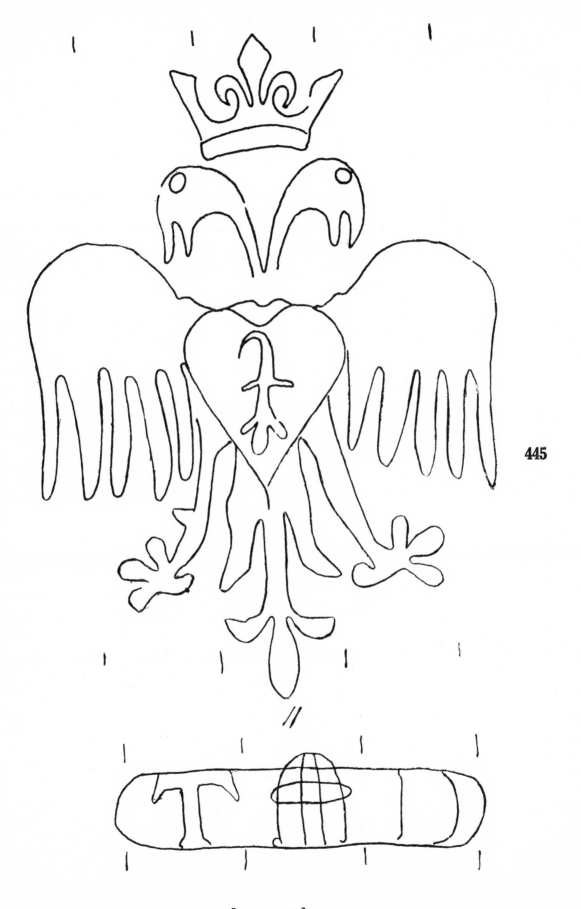

445

PASCAL LAMB

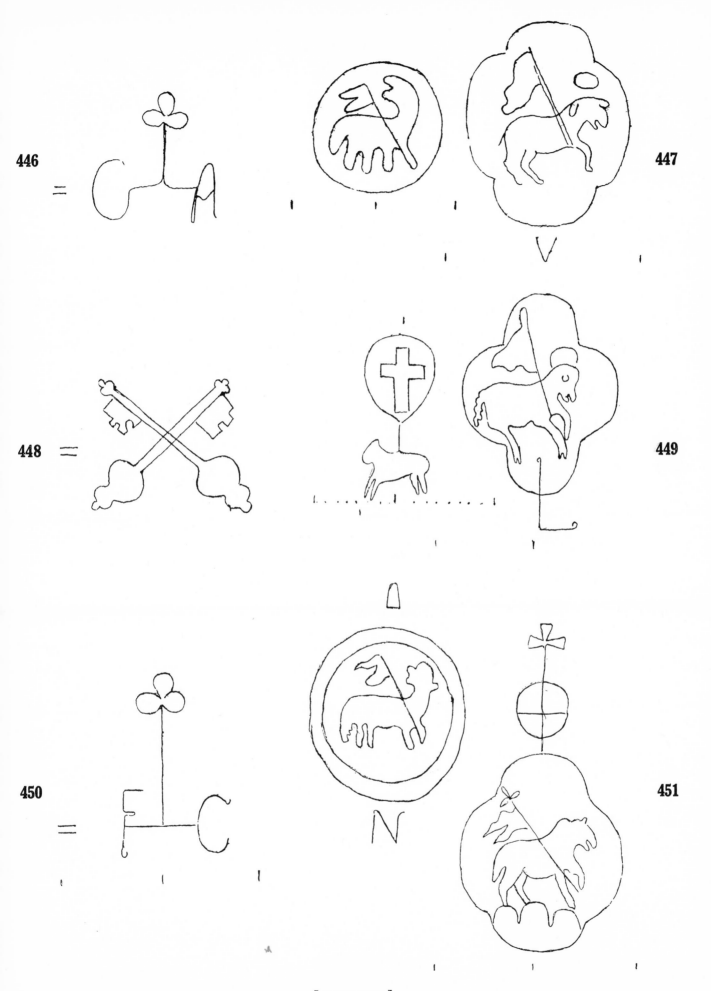

446

447

448

449

450

451

452

453

454

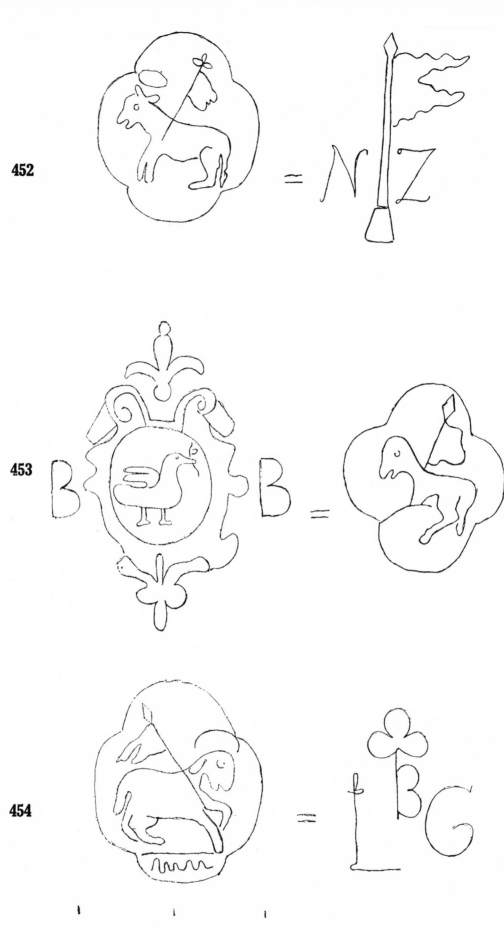

455

456

457

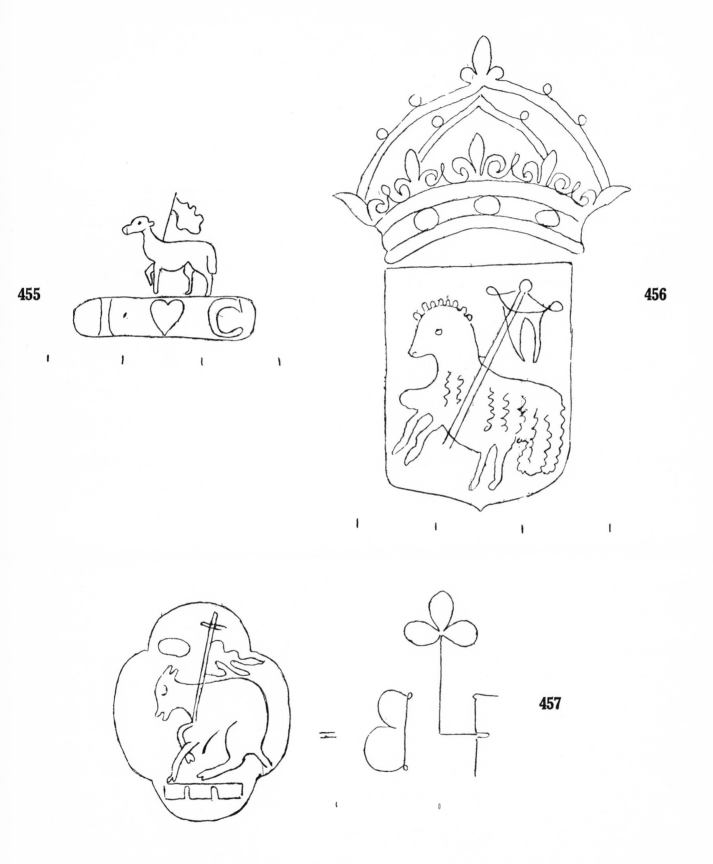

POT (GENERALLY FRENCH)

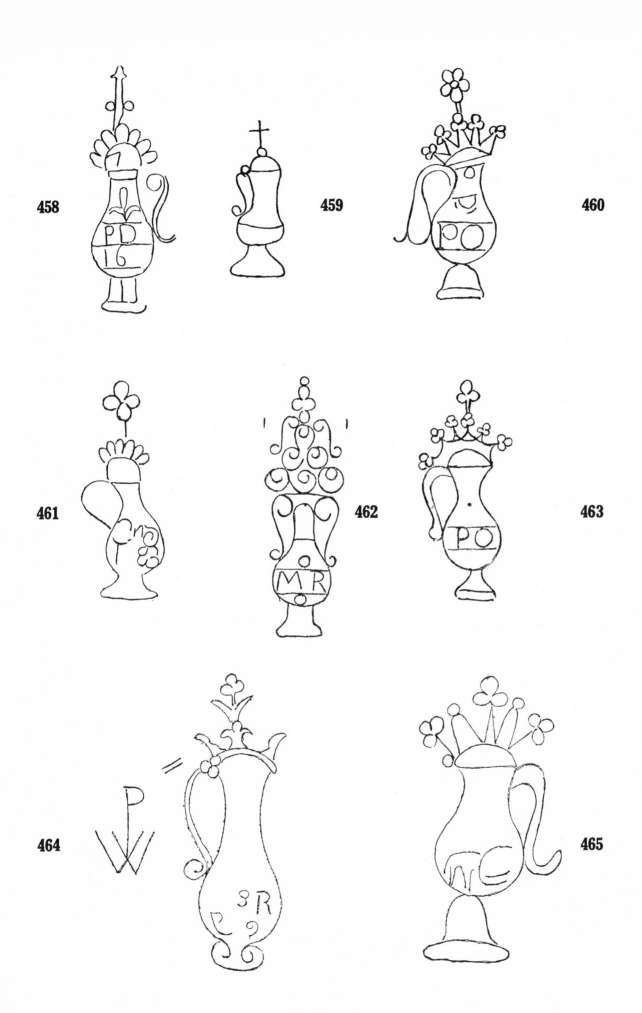

458 459 460

461 462 463

464 465

Watermarks in paper.

466

467

468

469

470

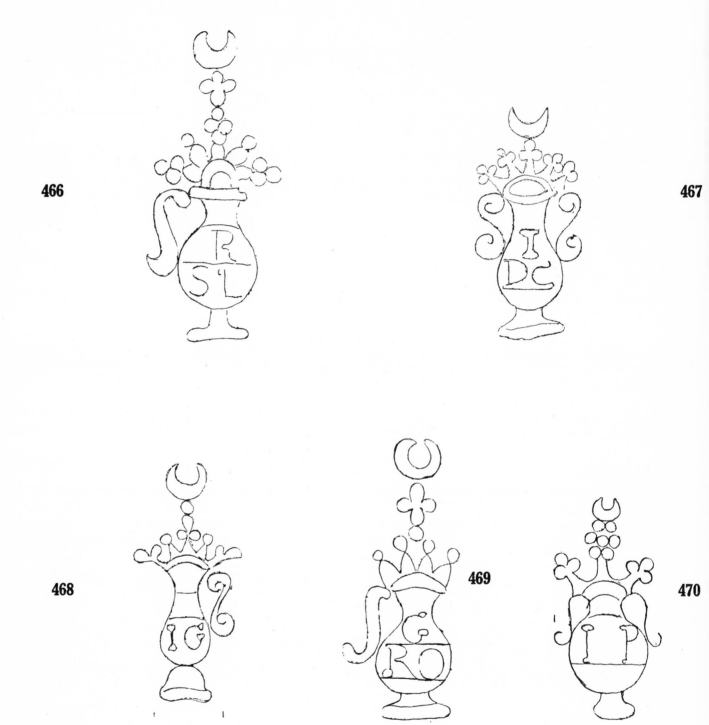

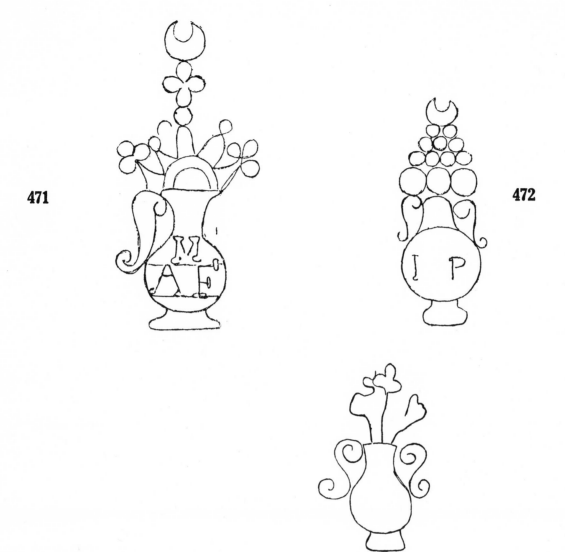

471

472

473

A ✠ GALHARDOИ

GRAPES (FRENCH)

474

475

476

DAVPHINE

477

A♡CARETTE

GNAB V

FIN

478

FINDE C☆RICHARD

AUVERGNE

M MATHIEU 479

A S^T PONS

[CCCLIII]

HATS

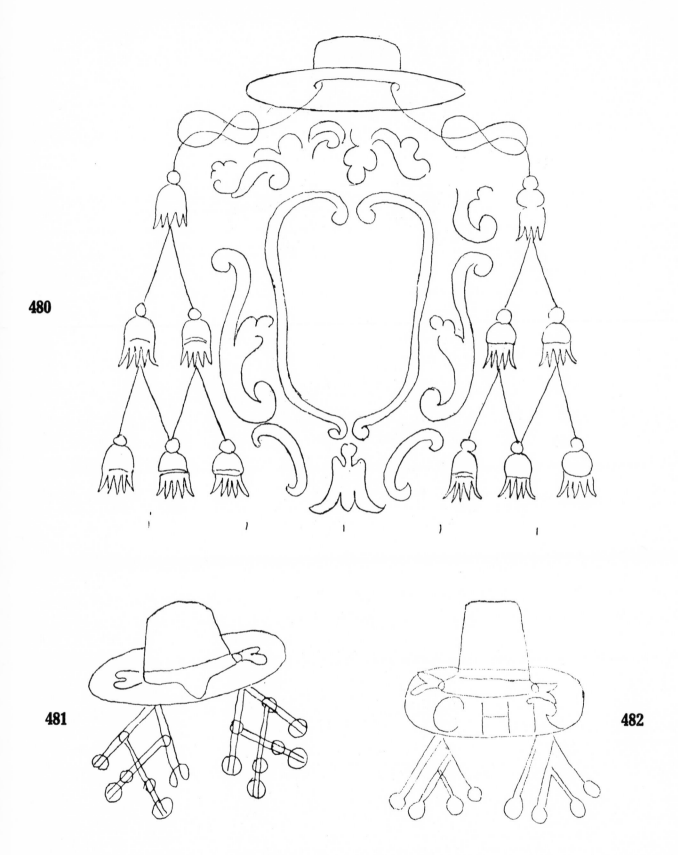

480

481

482

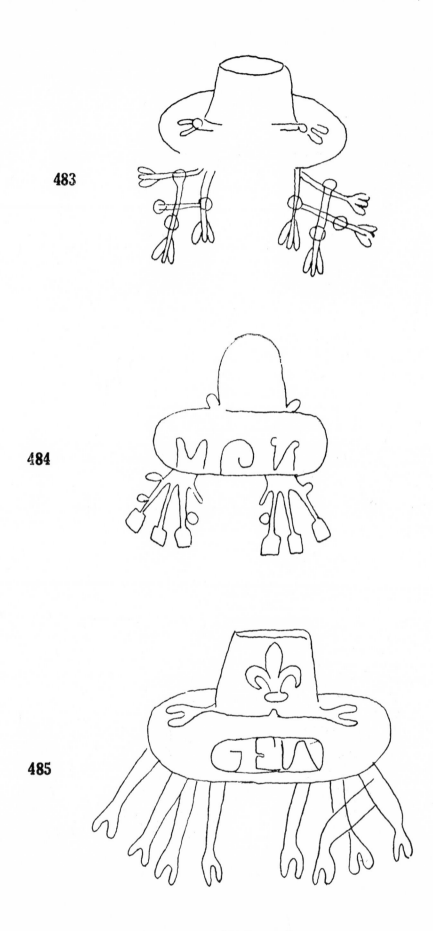

483

484

485

THREE HATS

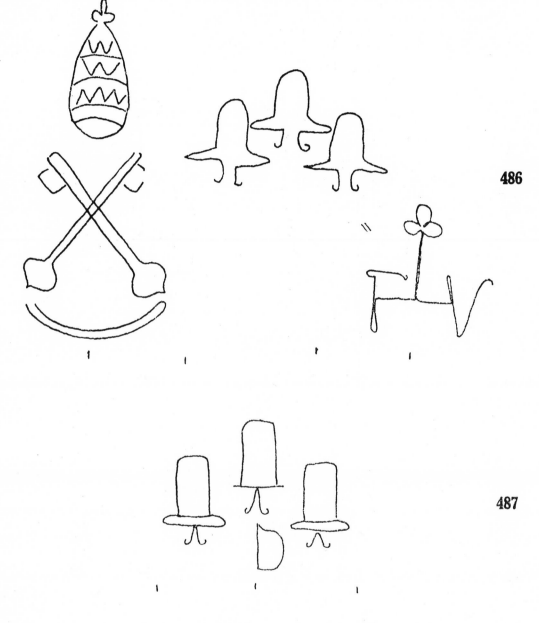

486

487

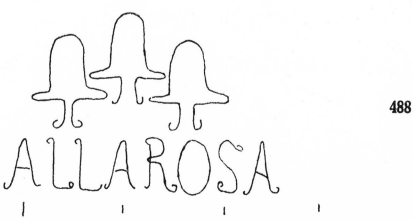

ALLAROSA

488

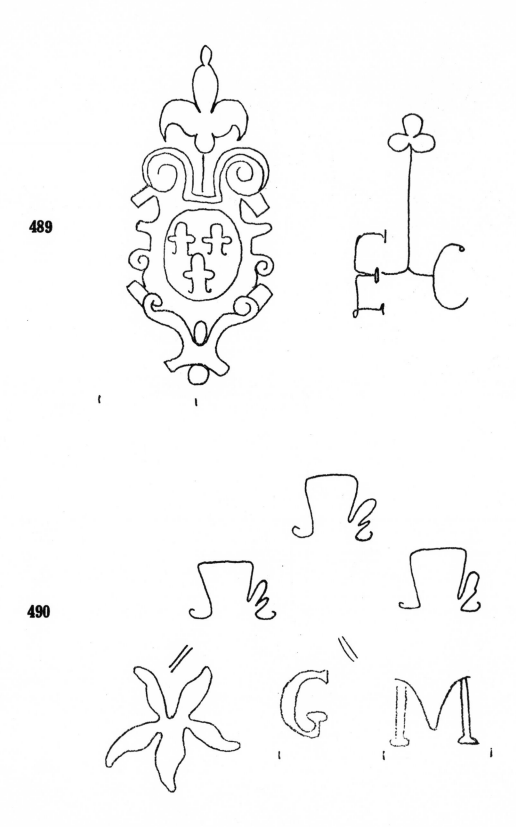

489

490

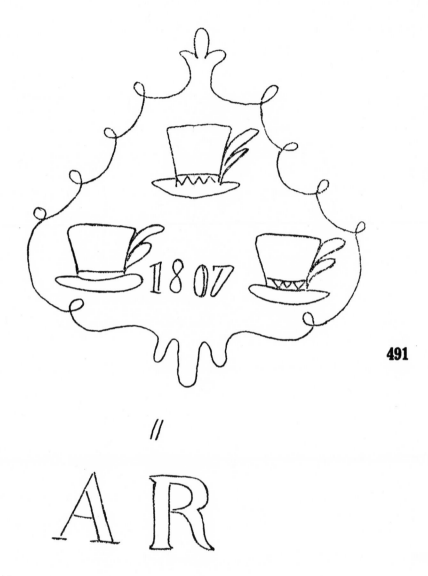

491

//

A R

ROYAL HEADS (FRENCH)

NAPOLEON EMPEREUR DES FRANÇAIS ROI D'ITALIE

492

493

494

MISCELLANEOUS

495

D. PAP. MOOLE

496

DE HAES

497

DEHAES

498

DEHAES

499

500

//

P R

501

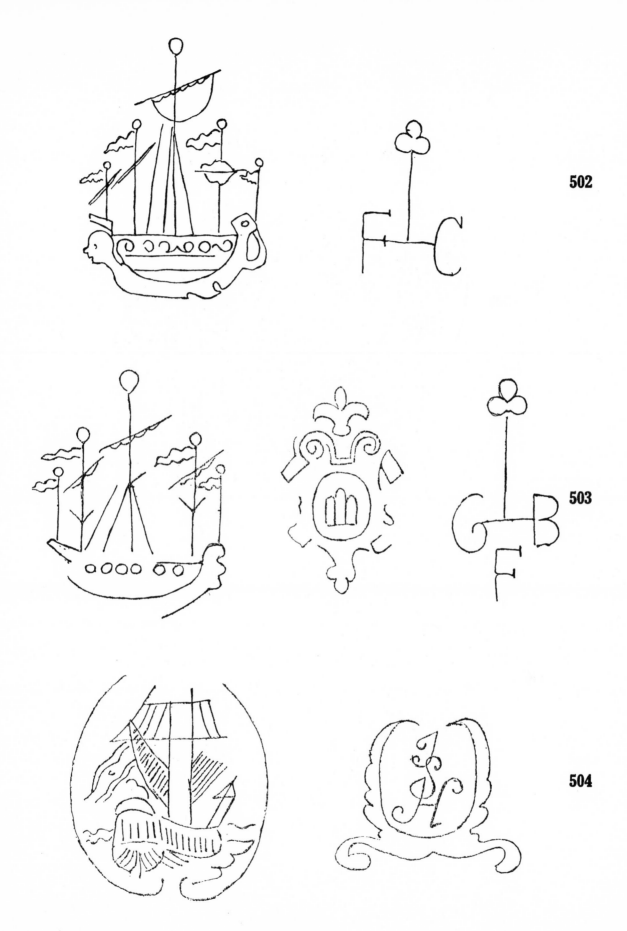

502

503

504

505

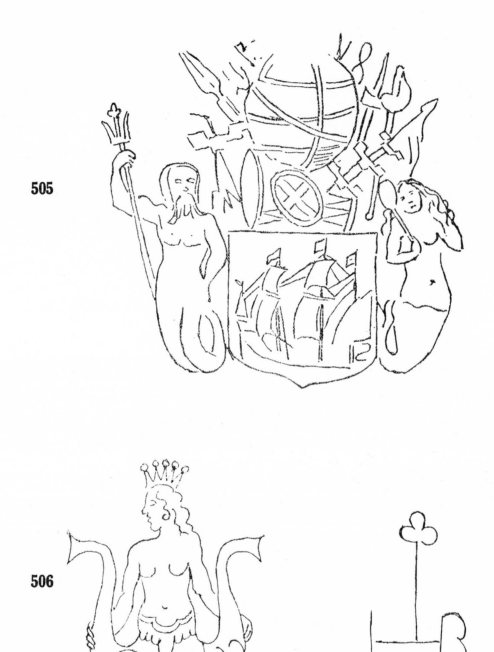

506

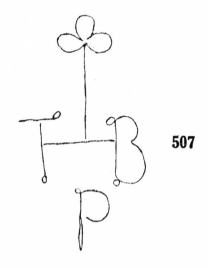

507

FARRERAS

508

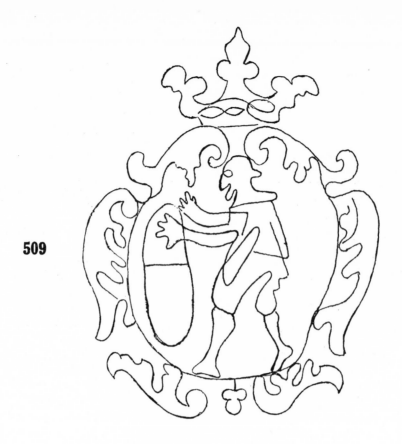

509

510

511

512

[CCCLXXIX]

513

514

[CCCLXXX]

515

516

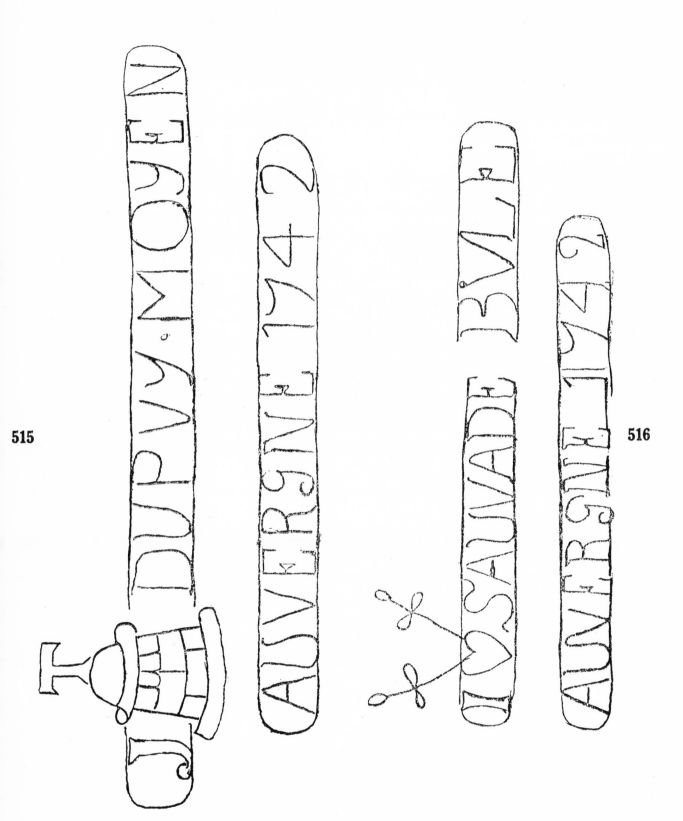

517

EXTRAORDINARIS
PUYKS PAPIERE

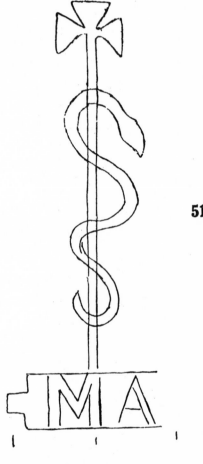

518

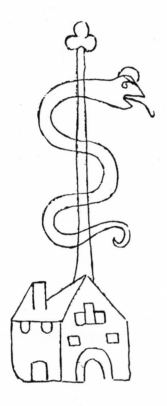

521

522

523

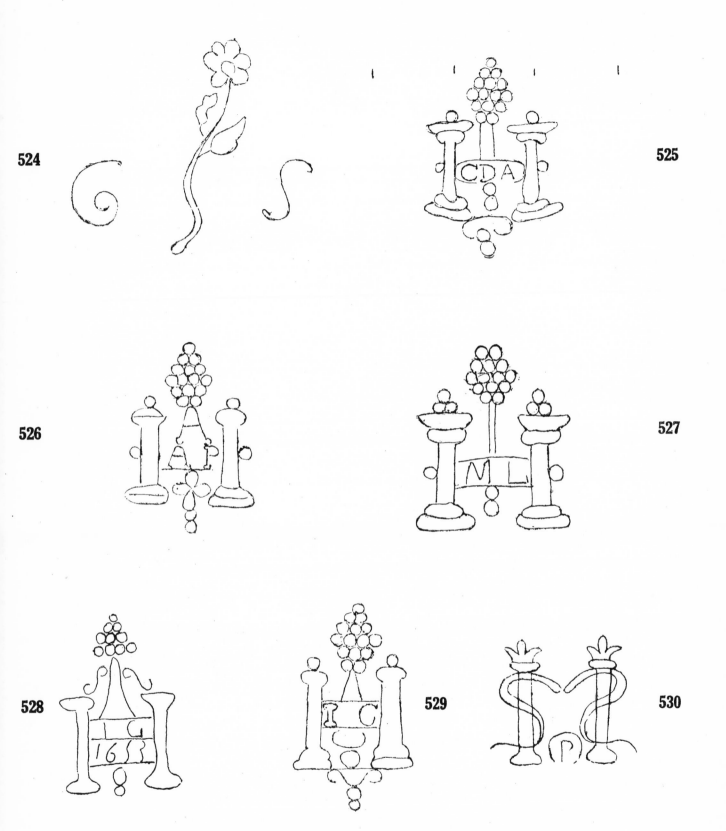

524   525

526   527

528   529   530

Watermarks in paper.

531

532

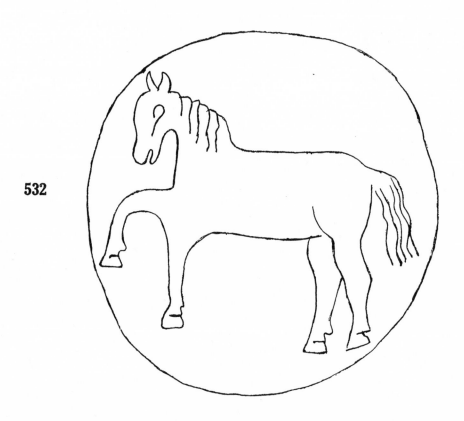

533

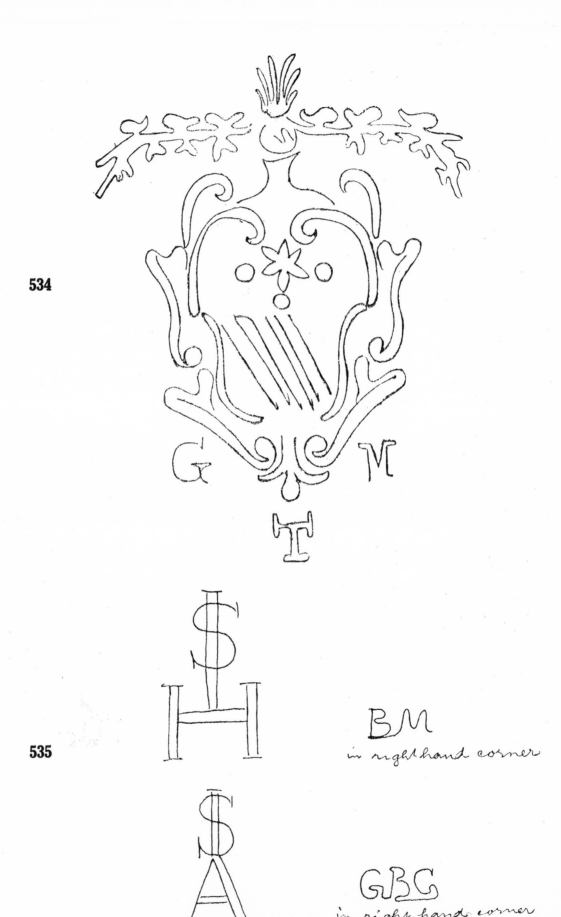

534

535

BM
in right hand corner

GBG
in right hand corner

INITIALS

536

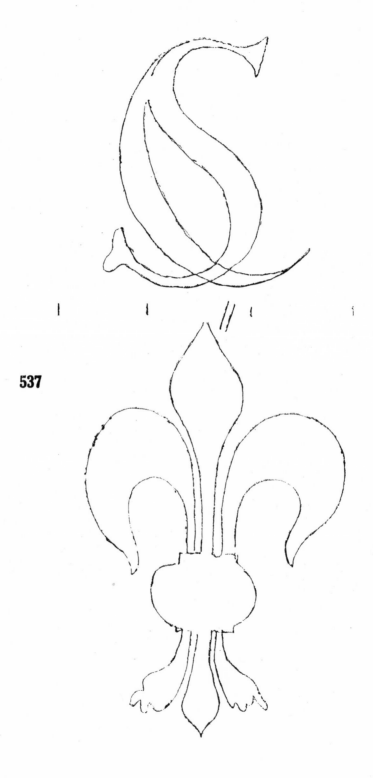

537

538

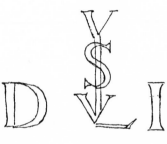

539

540

Watermarks in paper.

UNDETERMINED (FRENCH)

B BRUIN
FIN
DANGOUMOIS

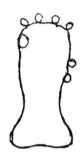

B BRUN
MOTEN
DANGOUMOIS

543

P TOMAS
MOYEN
DANGOUMOIS

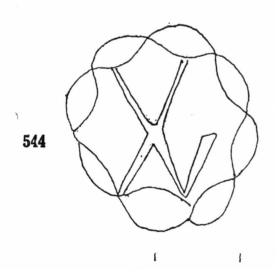

544

545

OFFICIAL STAMPED PAPER

546

FRENCH IMITATIONS
OF GENOESE WATERMARKS

547

R JARDEL
FIN
PERIGORD
1742

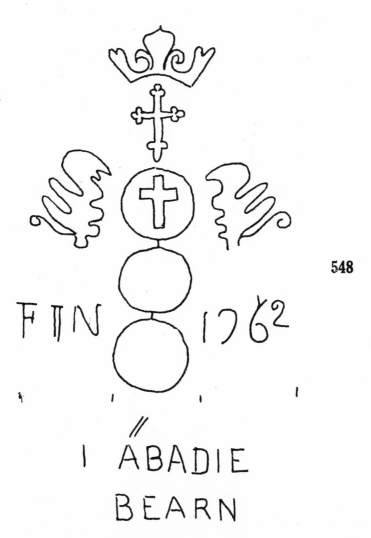

548

FIN 1762

I ABADIE
BEARN

[CDV]

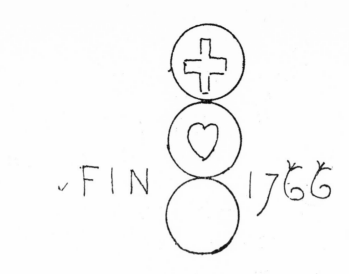

549

//

D·P·MONIE

BICORRE

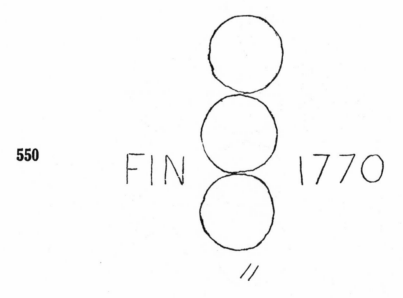

550

//

M RACUETTE

BEARNE

COUNTERMARKS AT EACH
CORNER OF PAPER

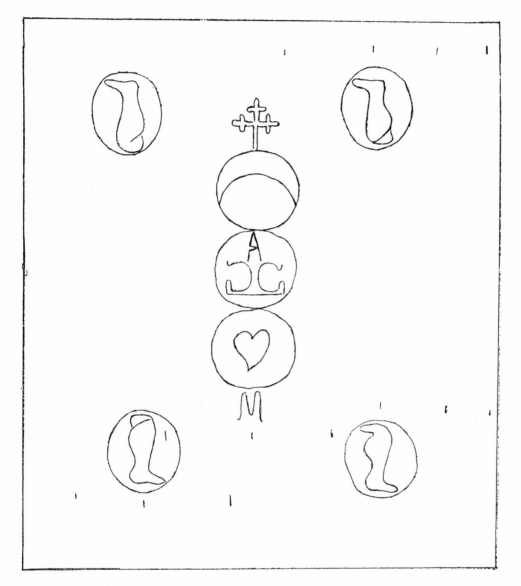

551

[CDIX]

552

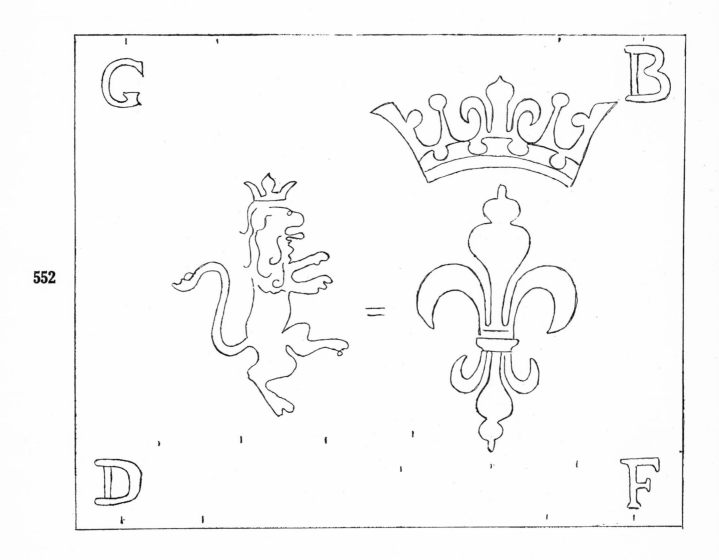

DOUBLE CHAIN WATERMARKS

554

553

555

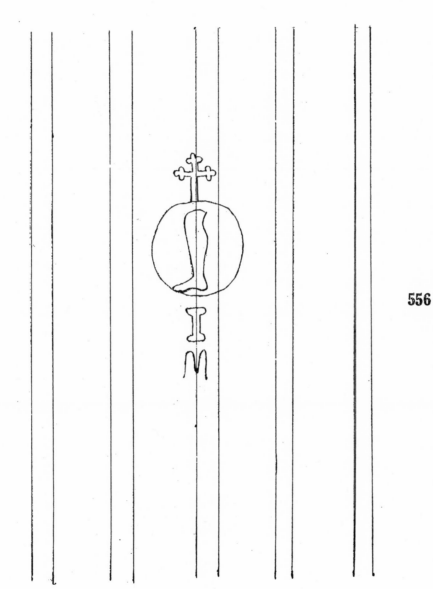

556

557

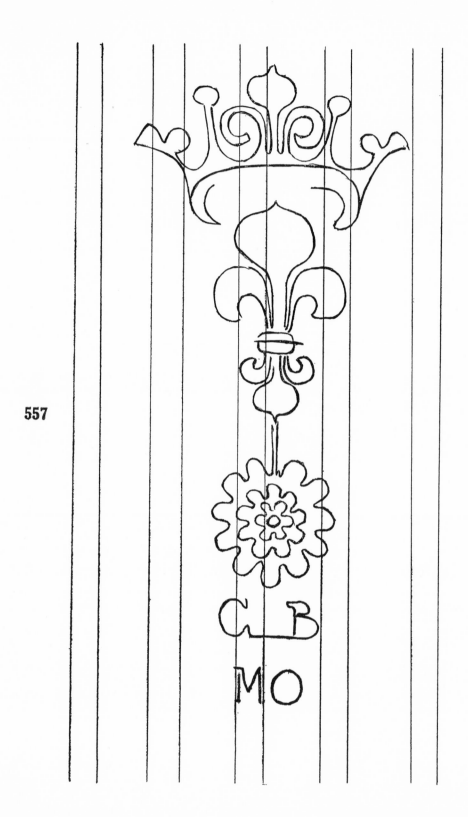

DATED PAPER

558

559

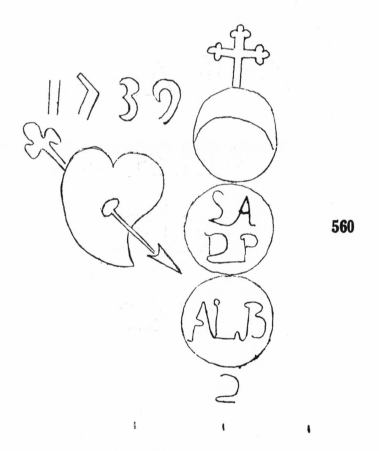

560

561

562

FIN DE
PAPETERIE ROYAL
EN ALSACE
1741

AORANGE
DAUPHINE
FIN
1742

563

564

565

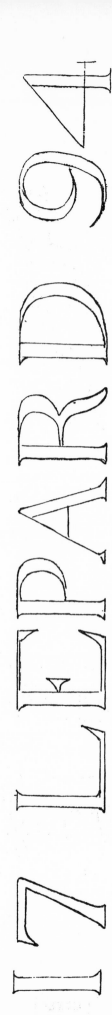

17 LEPARD 94

WATERMARKS IN ALLUSION
TO SURNAMES OF PAPER-MAKERS

566

567

Papier Bulles
de
T · D

568

569

GAG

570

TESTA

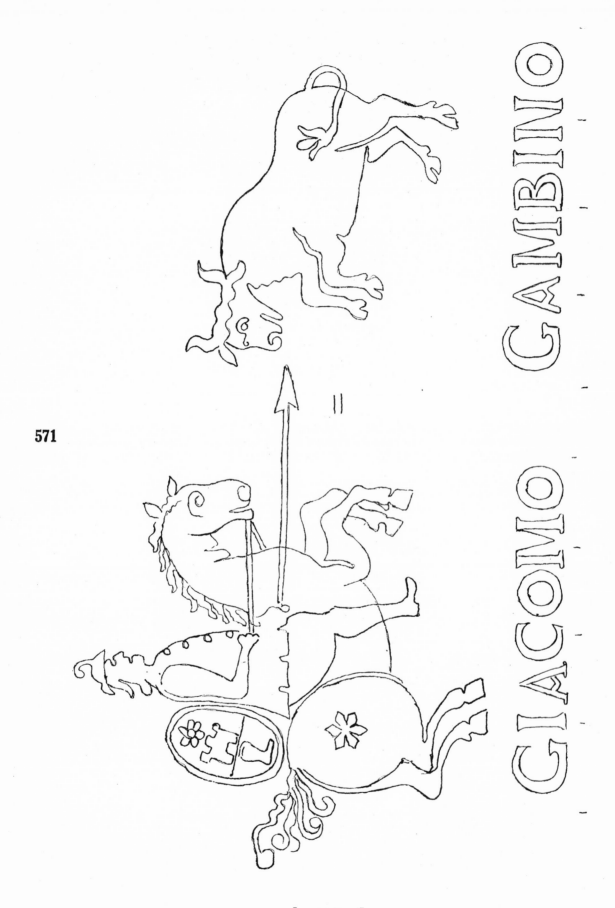

571

GIACOMO GAMBINO

[CDXXVIII]

572

573

ADRIAAN ROGGE

LEVEIRATTO

574

NICOLASLEBE

575

VH

PORRATA-

GAR

576

577

578

=

GIUSTI

THIS book is a striking example of what a layman can achieve by means of perseverance, research, and patience. About fifty years ago Mr. Churchill, then British Consul at Amsterdam, became, quite by chance, interested in paper marks. He began to collect tracings of watermarks found in public documents in the Amsterdam Municipal Archives, and sheets of old paper, including a number of rather rare ream wrappers. His subsequent examination of these papers led to the history of their makers and so the author found that Dutch traders, not being able to obtain sufficient home-made paper for their export markets - particularly England - went to France. There they financed manufacturers of paper, eventually even buying French mills, to make paper with Dutch marks, of which the *Pro Patria* and the *Arms of Amsterdam* are the most typical. This work contains a wealth of information on this point, due to the author's pioneer research, as shown by the evidence of nearly 600 watermarks reproduced in their original sizes, together, wherever possible, with details on the makers and date and place of manufacture.

This book, first published in 1935, almost simultaneously with NICOLAI, seems to have paved the way for a renewed interest in filigranology. In the 1950s and early 1960s several important studies appeared and at the same time the demand for Mr. Churchill's work grew. Hence it was reprinted in 1965, within two years followed by the present - unchanged - reprint.

The illustration on this jacket shows a seventeenth-century fascia from the Netherlands, depicting various stages of the manufacture of paper. Bottom row, from right to left: the pulping of rags in the water-driven mill; the actual laying of the paper in moulds, and the drying of finished sheets under pressure. The top row of panels shows, from left to right, wrapping of reams, selecting rags, and drying of new-made sheets.